ISLAMIC LAW
IN THE MODERN WORLD

J. N. D. ANDERSON

ISLAMIC LAW
in the MODERN WORLD

GREENWOOD PRESS, PUBLISHERS
WESTPORT, CONNECTICUT

340.59
A547i
1975

Library of Congress Cataloging in Publication Data

Anderson, James Norman Dalrymple.
    Islamic law in the modern world.

    Reprint of the ed. published by New York Univer-
sity Press, New York.
    Bibliography: p.
    1. Islamic law.   I.   Title.
Law   340.5'9   75-31816
ISBN 0-8371-8451-7

Originally published in 1959 by New York University Press, New York

Reprinted in 1975 by Greenwood Press
A division of Congressional Information Service
88 Post Road West, Westport, Connecticut 06881

Library of Congress Catalog Card Number 75-31816

ISBN 0-8371-8451-7

Printed in the United States of America

10 9 8 7 6 5 4

PREFACE

The School of Law of New York University was fortunate in the fall of 1958 to have as visiting member of its faculty Dr. J. N. D. Anderson, Professor of Oriental Laws in the University of London and Head of the Department of Law, School of Oriental and African Studies, University of London. Professor Anderson is universally acclaimed as one of the leading English-speaking authorities on Islamic Law.

In view of the heightened interest in the Middle East, especially among American businessmen and their legal advisers, the faculty of the School of Law thought that it would be a public service to invite Professor Anderson to give a series of lectures for the benefit of the interested members of the legal and business community. Because of the high quality of the lectures and the interest that was manifested by those who heard them, the faculty decided to publish the lectures for a wider audience. They were prepared for oral presentation and they are now printed substantially in that form. It is hoped that the lectures as delivered will prove to be more readable than they would be if recast as law review articles or as chapters in a treatise.

There is a very great need for understanding the legal system, the traditions, and the culture of the Middle Eastern countries by men of good will everywhere. It is the hope of the faculty of the School of Law that this book will contribute to this understanding.

RUSSELL D. NILES
Dean, New York University
School of Law

CONTENTS

INTRODUCTION

I. *The Need*

After thirteen centuries of accomplishment during which the Shari'a, or Sacred Law of Islam, has governed the lives of myriads of Muslims in successive generations, that great system of law is still the object of careful study by scholars and jurists in the East and the West. This is partly because, in the words of a Western orientalist, the Muslim jurists and theologians of the second century of the Hegira have "elaborated a structure of law that is, from the point of view of logical perfection, one of the most brilliant essays of human reasoning."[1] Another reason, which J. N. D. Anderson explains so well in the first of his present lectures, is that, according to Muslim concepts, the closest ties exist between religion and law. Islam is a complete way of life; a religion, an ethic, and a legal system all in one. To quote another Western authority, the Shari'a "permeated almost every side of social life and every branch of Islamic literature, and it is no exaggeration to see in it,

[1] H. A. R. Gibb, *Mohammedanism, An Historical Survey* (2d ed.; Oxford, 1953), p. 90.

in the words of one of the most penetrating of modern students of the subject, 'the epitome of the true Islamic spirit, the most decisive expression of Islamic thought, the essential kernal of Islam.' "[2]

However, the spiritual, cultural, and legal merits of Muslim law are by no means the only reasons why it is studied with such painstaking effort. The main reason for continuing interest in Muslim law is the fact that to more than four hundred million Muslims in Asia, Africa, and Europe, the Shari'a still forms an important part of the living law. No wonder that Edouard Lambert, the founder of the relatively modern science of comparative law, and more recently, René David of the law faculty of the University of Paris, should deal with the Shari'a as one of the leading systems of law in the world today.[3]

However, interest in the study of the Shari'a is not confined to Muslim jurists or students of comparative law. Thanks to closer cultural and economic relations with Islamic peoples and a growing sense of interdependence among nations, Western lawyers are becoming increasingly aware of the importance of getting better acquainted with the teaching of the Divine Law of Islam. The West owes more than it ordinarily realizes to the jurists who elaborated the principles of Muslim law. In the words of an eminent Italian jurist, D. de Santillana:[4]

Among our positive acquisitions from Arab law, there are legal institutions such as limited partnership (qirad), and

[2] *Ibid.,* p. 106, and G. Bergsträsser, *Grundzüge des Islamischen Rechts,* ed. Joseph Schacht, p. 1.

[3] See also Arminjon, Nolde, and Wolff, *Traité de droit comparé,* Vol. II.

[4] *Law and Society in the Legacy of Islam,* ed. Sir Thomas Arnold and Alfred Guillaume (Oxford, 1931), p. 310.

certain technicalities of commercial law. But even omitting these, there is no doubt that the high ethical standard of certain parts of Arab law acted favourably on the development of our modern concepts; and therein lies its enduring merit.

Furthermore, Islam is one of the three great monotheistic religions now engaged in the fight for the souls and minds of free men against the rising tide of atheistic historical materialism. Shortly before his death, in the foreword he wrote to the valuable work of Khadduri and Liebesny,[5] Associate Justice Robert H. Jackson of the Supreme Court of the United States, summed up as follows the reasons why Western lawyers should devote more attention to Muslim law:

> Today the anxious countries of the West find in the Islamic world some of their most bold and uncompromising allies in resisting the drive for world supremacy by those whose Prophet is Marx. We have become more objective about history and more tolerant of religious differences. Trade with the Middle East adds the element of expediency to other motives for study of its laws and institutions.

By way of illustration, I should like to add some footnotes to the foregoing text.

1. Shortly before he became Ambassador to Great Britain, Winthrop Aldrich paid a visit to Jeddah, where he met Sheikh Abdullah Al Soleiman, who was Minister of Finance of Saudi Arabia at that time. I well remember the following statement which Sheikh Abdullah made to his guest: "The United States can have confidence in our

[5] *Law in the Middle East,* ed. Majid Khadduri and Herbert J. Liebesny, Vol. 1, *Origin and Development of Islamic Law* (Washington, D.C.), p. viii.

mutually beneficial dealings, because our religion and our law are strongly opposed to communism, and because our word is our bond."

2. The picture of the late King Abdul Aziz Ibn Saud, the founder of modern Saudi Arabia, as he used to preside over his Mejlis is deeply impressed on my mind. On one memorable occasion he gave an audience to F. A. Davies, chairman of the Board of Directors of the Arabian American Oil Company (Aramco), in December, 1950. "Give me your hand, Mr. Davies," the King said; and then clasping Mr. Davies' extended hand, His Majesty said to him: "You can have confidence in us because our religion and our law make it our bounden duty to keep our compact with you. I have given you my pledge and my peace (*'ahdi wa amani*). You walk in the length and breadth of my land and enjoy the same security and protection as my own subjects."

3. The teaching of Muslim law, to which the King referred, expressed in the strongest language the two basic principles of freedom and sanctity of contract. These principles have received a striking application in a recent international award given in Geneva, Switzerland, on August 23, 1958. In conformity with the noble tradition of Muslim law, the state of Saudi Arabia and Aramco, parties to the Arbitration Agreement concluded in Jeddah on February 23, 1955, were in a position readily to agree on the following clause:

> Whereas the Government and Aramco state that (1) they respect all the obligations which they have undertaken and now undertake, (2) the Government and Aramco have never entertained the thought that they would not be bound by the agreements they have made and now make with one

another, and (3) agree that neither the Agreement on the part of the Government and Aramco to arbitrate the dispute herein pursuant to Article 31 of the Aramco Concession Agreement nor the arbitration itself includes or involves the right of sovereignty of the Government.

Even before the arbitration proceedings started, the parties recognized that the Aramco Concession Agreement, which they requested the tribunal to interpret, was their contractual law. This thought was forcefully expressed in the dictum in current use among Muslim and Middle Eastern lawyers: "Al-'aqd Shari'at al-muta'aqqidin" (The contract is the Shari'a or sacred law of the contracting parties).[6]

4. The vitality of Muslim law and its capacity to meet the exigencies of changing patterns of life have been dramatically demonstrated in the award of the arbitration tribunal referred to in the preceding paragraph. One of the most important findings of that tribunal was that a modern oil concession agreement was a valid contract, which was equally binding on the parties to it according to the principles of the Shari'a. The tribunal found that in submitting the dispute to arbitration, the state of Saudi Arabia had no desire "that its sovereignty should be taken into consideration and should endanger the basic principle of equality of the Parties before the Tribunal." Then after quoting international decisions, such as the award of the Permanent Court of International Justice of August 17, 1923, in the Wimbledon Case,[7] the arbitration tri-

[6] Compare this with the French expression of the same principle in Article 1134 of the French Civil Code: "Les conventions légalement formées tiennent lieu de loi entre les parties contractantes." Also, Sanhouri, *Al-Wasit, a Commentary on the New Egyptian Civil Code,* the Sources of Obligations, Masadir al-Iltizam (Cairo), p. 624.

[7] P. C. I. J., Series A, No. 1.

bunal added that it "would like to emphasize that the fore-going concept of sovereignty, which is the basis of this part of its decision, does not conflict with the teaching of Muslim law on this subject."

It is noteworthy that the award of August 23, 1958, referred to several works on Muslim law, ancient and modern, and borrowed heavily from Laoust, Nallino, Milliot, and Ibn Taimiya.[8]

The tribunal described the legal system of Saudi Arabia in the following terms:

> According to the doctrine and the information submitted by both Parties to the Tribunal, Saudi Arabia belongs to one of the great legal systems of the world, namely Muslim law, in which several rites or Schools are distinguished. The principal Sunni Schools are the Hanafi, the Malaki, the Shaffei and the Hanbali School. They do not differ in fundamentals but disagree in several points of detail.
>
> "The Hanbali School is followed by the Wahabis of Saudi Arabia. It is the School of Imam Ahmed ibn Hanbal (164–211 a.h., corresponding to 745–792 of the Christian era).

Applying the teaching of the Hanbali school, the arbitration tribunal came to the conclusion that the Imam, that is, the King, could "resort to a regime of mining concessions, 'in specie' of oil concessions, based on a contract, provided that this solution is not contrary to the rules of the Shari'ah." Then the tribunal went on to say:

[8] Henri Laoust, *Essai sur les doctrines sociales et politiques de Taki-D-Din Ahmed B. Taimiya* (Cairo, 1939); Nallino, *Raccolta di Scritti editi ed inediti*, t I, *l'Arabia Saoudiana;* Milliot, *Introduction à l'étude du droit musulman* (Paris, 1953); *Traité de droit public d'Ibn Taimiya, traduction annotée de la Siyasa Shari'ah* (Beyrouth, 1948).

The concession contract does not conflict with these rules, since it is in conformity with two fundamental principles of the whole Muslim system of law, i.e., the principle of liberty to contract within the limits of Divine Law, and the principle of respect for contracts. The first principle is stated by Ibn Taimiya as follows: "The following rule shall be obeyed: men shall be permitted to make all the transactions they need, unless these transactions are forbidden by the Book or by the Sunna." (Laoust, le Traité de droit public d'Ibn Taimiya, traduction annotée de la Siyasa Shari'ah, Beyrouth, 1948, p. 167; Milliot, op. cit., p. 205, who stresses the principle of freedom to contract, as one of the basic rules of the Law of Obligations in Islam.) The second basic rule, in Ibn Taimiya's opinion, results from the fact that Muslim Law does not distinguish between a treaty, a contract of public or administrative law and a contract of civil or commercial law. All these types are viewed by Muslim jurists as agreements or pacts which must be observed since God is a witness to any contract entered into by individuals or by collectivities; under Muslim Law, any valid contract is obligatory, in accordance with the principles of Islam and the Law of God as expressed in the Koran: "Be faithful to your pledge to God when you enter into a pact" (Laoust, Essai sur les doctrines sociales et politiques de Taki-D-Din Ahmed B. Taimiya, Le Caìre, 1939, p. 445).

There can be no stronger evidence of the importance of Muslim law wherever East meets West than these findings based on its teaching. They do not come from a Qadi's court sitting in Damascus or Baghdad in the times of the Umayyad or Abbasside caliphs, but from a modern tribunal in an international arbitral proceeding that took place very recently in a Western neutral country.

II. *The Fulfillment*

As the function creates the machinery necessary for its fulfillment, it was natural that the study of Muslim law in the West should have started much earlier in Great Britain, France, Holland, Germany, and Italy than it did in the Western Hemisphere. This was due to the earlier contacts established with the Turks in Europe; and later on between other Muslim peoples and the powers that became responsible for the rule of vast Muslim territories in Asia and Africa. Today these contacts are happily based on the much more satisfactory principles of the Charter of the United Nations, the interdependence of all free nations and their mutually beneficial co-operation in the pursuit of peace and happiness for all mankind.

Before World War I the study of Muslim law was diligently pursued in the universities of Western Europe. In the United States the same need for better acquaintance with Muslim law began to be felt when economic relations with the Middle East became increasingly important.

However, apart from some learned American scholars, who were concerned with Muslim culture in general rather than with Muslim law in particular, it was only as late as 1948 that the interest of practicing lawyers in the United States was aroused in the study of the Shari'a. Under the auspices of the Arabian American Oil Company, a group of lawyers met in Lenox, Massachusetts, in September, 1948, to discuss Muslim law. Joseph Schacht, then of Oxford University and now of Leyden University, came from overseas and gave several addresses on the Shari'a. This was the first time for a conference on Muslim law to meet on American soil.

It is a tribute to the wisdom of the great King Abdul Aziz Ibn Saud that he foresaw the need, and advised George W. Ray, Jr., general counsel of the Arabian American Oil Company, to take the necessary steps to meet it. The story of the conversation between the King and Ray had better be told in Ray's own words:

> When I first joined Aramco, I had the great pleasure of talking to the former King, one of the greatest men I have ever known. Since I was a lawyer, we naturally began to talk about the law. . . . He said he would advise me to get some young American men and send them to schools where they could study Muslim law because that was the law of his country. Then he proceeded to tell me for an hour or so about the various versions of Muslim law and concluded with the statement that if I could get these young men to study the teaching of the Hanbali school, I would have experts in the law of Saudi Arabia.
>
> Now that was an experience of the finest I ever had. I took His Majesty's advice. It was within a short time after that conversation that we had some of our young American men going to the universities to study the Hanbali law. They are all fine young men.

The brilliant young lawyers to whom Ray was referring in his conversation with the King have had to be sent to Oxford, London, and Paris. Today several seats of learning in the United States are giving regular courses in Muslim law.

III   *The Lectures*

It was my privilege to attend the lectures that J. N. D. Anderson of the University of London gave at the School of Law of New York University. It is gratifying to have these lectures available now in printed form.

In the East, as well as in the West, it was customary for works in highly specialized domains of knowledge to be written and published under the auspices of a powerful ruler. Thus the Imam Abu Yusuf, Chief Justice of Baghdad, wrote his classical work on taxation in Muslim law at the request and for the guidance of the Fifth Abbasside Caliph Harun al-Rashid. Again, a parallel to the compilation of the Corpus Juris Civilis of Roman law, which bears the name of the Emperor Justinian, can be found in Muslim law. Al Fatawa'l-Hindiya (the Indian opinions), a compilation of the teaching of the Hanafi school, bears the title: Al Fatawa'l-Alamkiriya, after the name of the Indian ruler under whose patronage this monumental work was produced.

It is a circumstance of happy augury that the publication of Anderson's lectures is not subsidized by any individual or learned institution. The patron of the present work is the legal profession in the United States, at whose request these lectures are now being published.

The Imam al-Shafi'i, founder of "Usul-ul-Fiqh," or the science of Muslim jurisprudence, mentions in the second or "Egyptian" version of his famous "Risala," or epistle, that when he traveled to Egypt, he had to leave some of his books behind him and therefore he had to rewrite his epistle in Egypt. It did not suffer for having been rewritten, and its Egyptian version is the authoritative one.[9] Anderson's knowledge of Muslim law is so profound and

[9] This episode is also referred to in Joseph Schacht's introduction to his work, *The Origins of Muhammadan Jurisprudence* (Oxford, 1950), p. vii.

accurate that his lectures likewise do not suffer from the fact that he delivered and wrote them away from London without access to his library.

Anderson writes from the vantage point of a scholar who is familiar with the sciences of jurisprudence and comparative law. But the great merit of his lectures is that they are not merely of academic or historical interest. He is more concerned with the practical side of Muslim law as applied today in various Islamic countries than with the pure science of "Fiqh," or Mohammedan jurisprudence. The Imam Ahmed Ibn Hanbal, one of the heads of the four Sunni or Orthodox schools of Muslim law, had traveled to the distant parts of Arabia in quest of "Hadiths," or Traditions of the Prophet. Anderson has likewise recently traveled far and wide in the course of a survey of the application of Islamic law in the British colonial territories in Africa and in the Colony and Protectorate of Aden. In 1950 and 1951 he visited Tanganyika, Nyasaland, Zanzibar, Kenya, Uganda, British Somaliland, the Colony and Protectorate of Aden, Nigeria, the Gold Coast (Ghana), Gambia, and Sierra Leone.[10] Since then he has paid three more visits to some of these countries, most recently as a member of the Panel of Jurists appointed by the Northern Nigerian government, to advise on their legal and judicial systems. In addition he has traveled widely and lived for some years in the Middle East. He gives us up-to-date information on the reform movement of the Muslim family law in Egypt, Syria, Tunisia, Algeria, and Morocco. One of the fascinating

[10] See the publication of the Colonial Office, J. N. D. Anderson, *Islamic Law in Africa* (London, 1954), Colonial Research Publication No. 16.

features of the present lectures is the description of the methods used to adapt Muslim family law to the exigencies of the new pattern of social and economic life, and to enact the badly needed reforms. It is a tribute to the vitality, resourcefulness, and flexibility of the Muslim system of law that it was possible to introduce these substantial changes in the law while still preserving its spirit intact.

Since Muslim law is such a basic factor of Muslim thinking, these lectures constitute a step forward toward better understanding and more friendly relations with the Muslim world. By the same token, they serve the cause of world peace.

DR. SABA HABACHY, K.B.E.

New York
March, 1959

ISLAMIC LAW
IN THE MODERN WORLD

.1.

CONCEPTIONS OF LAW:
ISLAMIC AND WESTERN

I should like to begin by saying what a pleasure it is, and what an honor I consider it to be, to be asked to give this series of lectures under the auspices of New York University School of Law. It was only some eighteen months ago that I paid my first visit to this country, having previously always traveled East rather than West; but I enjoyed this experience so much that when an invitation came to spend some three months as visiting professor, dividing my time between the Department of Oriental Studies at Princeton University and this law school, I was eager to accept.

You will understand, however, that I approach this series of lectures with some diffidence, for it is inevitable that my audience, distinguished though it obviously is, should come from extremely varied backgrounds. Some are experts in English law or jurisprudence, but with little or no knowledge of the law of Islam, while others are experts in the Middle East or some other part of the Muslim world, but not lawyers. So I trust that all will pardon me if part of what I say to you may appear somewhat obvious and commonplace.

Now in any consideration of Islamic law, even for the most practical of purposes—and, not least, in any consideration of the place it holds in the modern world—it is essential initially to understand the nature and ethos of that law, radically different as they are from Western concepts. That is why for my first lecture I have chosen the subject "Conceptions of Law—Islamic and Western."

There can be no doubt that the first, and basic, and most obvious distinction of all between the two systems—the distinction that obtrudes itself on the most superficial approach to the subject—is that Western law, as we know it, is essentially secular, whereas Islamic law is essentially religious. But merely to say this is to express the fundamental difference in a wholly inadequate way.

As you will all know, the law of continental Europe looks back, generally speaking, to Roman law. And Roman law, of course, received its most authoritative articulation under Justinian, when the empire was already officially Christian. But the Justinian legislation itself looked back to the great jurists of the Antonine era, who wrote at a time when the old paganism had already lost its hold over educated men, yet before the influence of Christianity had taken its place. Essentially, then, Roman law represents a law devised by men for men, a masterpiece of mature legal deliberation. It was therefore a law that could be changed, if circumstances so required, in much the same way in which it had been formulated.

This is the heritage of the civil law countries today. In these countries we find a legal system based on codes derived in large part from Roman law, as enacted by emperor or legislature, although interpreted and applied, of course, by the courts. It is a human, secular law that can easily be changed by the same authority that enacted it. And much the same applies fundamentally to the law of Britain and America. Here the common law is in the ascendant, and the case law of the courts assumes a dominant position, although legislation is today assuming an ever greater importance. However this may be, it is a secular, human law that can easily be changed by the legislature, with the proviso, of course, that in this country the Supreme Court may always strike down any ordinary legislation as contrary to the Constitution.

But Islamic law (and to a lesser extent many other legal systems of the Orient) is essentially different, for it is regarded fundamentally as divine law—and, as such, as basically immutable.

To the Muslim there is indeed an ethical quality in every human action, characterized by *qubh* (ugliness, unsuitability) on the one hand or *husn* (beauty, suitability) on the other. But this ethical quality is not such as can be perceived by human reason; instead, man is completely dependent in this matter on divine revelation. Thus all human actions are subsumed, according to a widely accepted classification, under five categories: as commanded, recommended,[1] left legally indifferent, reprehended, or else prohibited by Almighty God. And it is only in regard to the middle category (i.e., those things which are left

[1] I.e., one who acts accordingly may expect to be rewarded, but one who does not will not be punished, in the next world. The same principle applies, *mutatis mutandis,* in regard to what is "reprehended."

legally indifferent) that there is in theory any scope for human legislation.

But this fact leads directly to the second basic difference between these two systems of law, namely, that Islamic law is enormously wider in its scope than Western law. To the Western mind, law—in the lawyer's sense—may be defined for our immediate purpose as what is, or at least might be, enforced by the courts. Islamic law, on the contrary, takes the whole of human conduct for its field. If you consult any of the classical compendiums of law, you will find that they deal first—in the vast majority of cases—with such questions as ritual purity, prayer, fasting, almsgiving, and pilgrimage; next, it may be, with family law (i.e., marriage, divorce, paternity, guardianship, and succession); then, perhaps, with the law of contract, of civil wrongs, and of what we should call crimes; while they also deal with such questions as the law of peace and war, the law of evidence and procedure, and with a multitude of other subjects such as the circumstances in which an invitation to a wedding may properly be refused. It thus covers every field of law—public and private, national and international—together with an enormous amount of material that we in the West would not regard as law at all.

A Muslim may indeed consult his lawyer, just as a Westerner might, as to how he can avoid trouble with the courts or safeguard his financial interests; but he may also look to him for religious and ethical advice, and for guidance as to what actions will, and what will not, please his Maker.[2]

[2] Cf. D. B. Macdonald, *Muslim Theology, Jurisprudence and Constitutional Theory* (New York, 1903), p. 73.

But it is obvious, of course, that much of this law could never in the very nature of things be enforced by human courts. It is only, for example, those actions which are specifically commanded or forbidden—not the intermediate categories of what is recommended, left legally indifferent, or reprehended—which could be so enforced; and we find a great deal, even within these two decisive categories, which is left, in so far as any sanction is concerned, to the bar of Eternity. It is readily understandable, then, to find that Islamic law has been aptly described as a "Doctrine of Duties."[3]

It may be helpful and suggestive if we next look at this law with the eye of a student of Western theories of jurisprudence, although I myself cannot claim to be any expert in this field.

Let us take, in the first place, the Austinian theory. "The matter of Jurisprudence," Austin tells us, "is positive law: law, simply and strictly so called: or law set by political superiors to political inferiors."[4] But can this theory possibly be applied to Islamic law? The answer seems clear that it can be so applied only if the "political superior" of the definition is conceived in terms of Almighty God, who will enforce this law in such manner as He sees fit.

Or take, in the second place, Hans Kelsen's "Pure Theory of Law" as another example of what may be termed the Imperative school. Jurisprudence, he assures us, is concerned with "law as it is, not as it should be."

[3] Cf. *Encyclopedia of Islam* II, 105 (I. Goldziher, quoting C. Snouck Hurgronje).

[4] J. Austin, *The Province of Jurisprudence Determined* (London, 1954), p. 9.

But in the Islamic theory (although not, of course, altogether in practice) precisely the contrary is true. Again, Kelsen defines law as a "system or hierarchy of norms which prescribe what always ought to happen in given circumstances"—all resting in the final analysis on the "basic norm" of the "first constitution" of the state concerned.[5] But this definition, equally obviously, can only be applied to Islamic law—in its jurisprudential theory— if we conceive this basic norm or first constitution in terms of the sovereignty of God and the authority of His revelation (as the Muslim regards it).

Let us turn, in the third place, to the Historical school of jurisprudence, if I may so term it. To the historical jurists law, like language, manners, and constitution, has no separate existence but is a simple function or facet of the whole life of a nation. In early times, we are told, the common conviction of the people is the origin of law; but, with the development of civilization, the making of law, like every other activity, becomes a distinct function, and is now exercised by the legal profession. So law "arises from silent, anonymous forces, which are not directed by arbitrary or conscious intention, but operate in the way of customary law."[6] But this theory, however true it may be of the way in which much of Islamic law did in fact evolve, is fundamentally incompatible with its basic concept and theory. It is, however, noteworthy in passing that the emphasis put by this school on the part played by the legal profession in the making of the law is par-

[5] H. Kelsen, *General Theory of Law and the State* (Cambridge, Mass., 1949), pp. 123 ff., 153.

[6] H. Kantorowicz, "Savigny and the Historical School of Law," in *Law Quarterly Review*, 53 (1937), 332 ff.

ticularly relevant to the way in which Islamic law was developed; for this law has always been a "lawyers' law" (based indeed not so much on the law of the courts as on the law of the textbooks, not so much on the decisions of judges as on the opinions of jurists); but a law which those lawyers always profess to have derived not from "silent, anonymous forces" or from the operations of customary law, but from the only reliable criterion of divine revelation.

Or take, in the fourth place, the Sociological school of jurisprudence. To the sociological jurists the paramount consideration is not so much the history of the law as the mutual influence of law and society. Now this again may represent an admirable picture of how Islamic law did in part develop in the pages of history; but it is radically incompatible with its juristic theory. For by that theory, it is clear, it is not society that influences law, but the law that provides a divinely revealed norm and standard to which Muslim society is under a perpetual duty to conform.

Or consider, in the fifth place, what we may term the American Realists, as exemplified in the famous words of Justice Holmes: "The prophecies of what the courts will do in fact, and nothing more pretentious, are what I mean by law."[7] Now this, no doubt, may be an apt definition of Islamic law as actually administered in this country or that; but it represents a definition which no Islamic jurist would tolerate for a moment as a description of the Shari'a—or Islamic law—as such. On the contrary, however far the courts may stray in practice from the right path,

[7] O. W. Holmes, "The Path of the Law" (1897), 10 *Harvard Law Review,* p. 461.

to the Muslim the Shari'a remains the Shari'a, the law which the courts ought to apply and which every individual is bound to obey.

Again, let us turn, in the sixth place, to the Swedish Realists. "The 'binding force' of law," Olivecrona assures us, "is a reality merely as an idea in human minds." This idea indeed may be said even to fulfill a "dangerous, reactionary and obscurantist function. It suggests to the human mind that law is something standing outside and above the facts of social life, that law has an independent validity of its own which is not man-made." The reality, he tells us, is that "law is made by men, that it exerts pressure on men, on the public and on policemen, and on judges."[8] But this attitude contrasts with the Islamic conception of the Shari'a most clearly and decisively of all. For to the Muslim the Shari'a does most certainly stand outside and above the facts of social life; it unquestionably has an independent validity of its own which is not man-made. Even if, moreover, it exerted pressure on no one at all, it would still remain the law which is divinely incumbent on all believers.

It is when we turn finally to the exponents of natural law that we find a far more congruous comparison. For the natural lawyers, like the Muslim jurists, conceive of law in terms of an eternal, transcendental norm to which mankind is of necessity required always to attempt to approximate. Yet even here there are certain fundamental differences between the two concepts which are, I think, deeply significant. I must confine myself in this context to two: first, that the natural lawyers conceive of that law

[8] K. Olivecrona, *Law as Fact* (Copenhagen, 1939), p. 17; G. B. J. Hughes, *Jurisprudence* (London, 1955), p. 162.

as being inherent in the very nature of things, in the universe, in the nature of rational creatures, and in the fundamental rights of man; and, second, that they also conceive of that law as being discernible—in large part—by human reason, which is competent to determine the general outline, at least, of natural justice. But when we turn to what I may term the dominant or central doctrine of Muslim orthodoxy, we find that neither of these propositions is in fact accepted; for the Ash'aris[9] deny not only that the human mind, apart from divine revelation, is capable of discerning the ethical quality in human actions, but even that such an ethical quality exists at all, apart from the divine command or prohibition. To them God does not command certain actions because they are intrinsically good, nor forbid certain behavior because it is inherently evil; instead, actions are good or bad exclusively because God commands or forbids them.

Yet this view, though dominant, was by no means undisputed in Islam. The Mu'tazalis,[10] for instance, took a very different position. To them all human behavior was intrinsically good or evil, and God commanded the good because it was good and forbade the evil because it was evil. Further, they held that in some cases human reason could indeed perceive—quite independently of any direct revelation—that an act was good or bad in itself; and in such cases revelation did no more than confirm this judgment of the human mind. In other cases, however, man

[9] The Ash'aris are the dominant school of scholastic theology in Islam.

[10] The Mu'tazalis were a party of sincere Muslims with certain rationalistic tendencies. They enjoyed a short period of dominance before being branded as heretical.

could not of himself perceive the inherent ethical quality in a certain course of conduct, and in such circumstances he was, of course, dependent on divine revelation for guidance. And although the Mu'tazalis were largely discredited by the passage of the years, others—such as the Maturidis[11] and many Hanafi jurists—shared their views in regard to these two propositions.

To review the position, then, it seems clear that the views of the Imperative school of jurisprudence can be applied to the Islamic conception only if Austin's "political superior" and Kelsen's "basic norm" and "first constitution" are interpreted in a theological sense; that the views of the Historical and Sociological schools, however much they may explain in part how Islamic law developed in history, are fundamentally incompatible with its jurisprudential theory; and that the assertions of the Realists—in their American and, still more, their Swedish varieties—are even more diametrically incompatible with the Islamic concept. The views of the Natural Law school, on the other hand, are much closer to the Islamic doctrine, but with certain significant differences. As for the place of human reason, the Muslim jurists accord this a vital role, as we shall see, in the deduction of substantive legal rules from the revealed sources, but virtually no place as a source from which the substantive law may itself be derived.

But enough, I think, of this jurisprudential comparison. It is time to look more closely at Islamic law itself and the sources from which it was in fact derived.

The first source of this law, as all Muslims would affirm,

[11] The Maturidis are a school of scholastic theology parallel to, but less popular than, the Ash'ari school.

is the Koran, which is regarded by the orthodox as the *ipsissima verba* of God, written from eternity in Arabic in heaven, and vouchsafed to the Prophet, as the need arose, through the agency of the Angel Gabriel. We even find Islamic law described at times—but always, I think, by non-Muslims—as the "law of the Koran." In point of fact, however, there are comparatively few verses in the Koran that are of any strictly legal significance. To describe the Shari'a as the "law of the Koran," therefore, is somewhat analogous to describing Roman law as the "law of the Twelve Tables," except that it is certainly true that some of the rules of Islamic law can be traced straight back to this fundamental source. All the same, Joseph Schacht has shown that the derivation of legal rules from the Koran was not so much primary (as the traditional theory, of course, asserts) as secondary; for these rules were not so much taken directly from the Koran *in abstracto* as from customary law and administrative practice, as these were confirmed, rejected, or amended by the jurists in the light of Koranic—or, indeed, general Islamic—teaching.[12]

In any case, the Koran alone could never have provided an adequate source for any legal system. So in the traditional view it was augmented from the very first by the Sunna or custom of the Prophet; for Sunni jurists maintain that when Mohammed died, the fount of divine revelation ceased to flow, and his community was left with the divine Book (which was soon compiled) and with the memory of how the Prophet had himself acted; and that

---

[12] Cf. J. Schacht, *Origins of Muhammadan Jurisprudence* (Oxford, 1950), pp. 190 ff.; also in *Law in the Middle East* (Washington, 1955), pp. 39 ff.

they used the latter to fill out the former. Again, however, Schacht and others have shown that this is more an idealized than a historical account of how Islamic law was developed at the beginning of the Muslim era, for in early years the science of traditions as to what the Prophet had said, done, or allowed—which were later held to authenticate his Sunna—was completely undeveloped. On the contrary, the term Sunna in its earliest connotations meant first the ancient customs of the Arabs and then the "living tradition" of the ancient schools of law.[13] But the situation underwent a radical change from around the end of the second century of the Muslim era, and specific traditions as to what Mohammed had said, had done, or had allowed to be done in his presence—most of them, beyond question, fabricated—came to be acknowledged as the second source of the Shari'a.

Yet even these traditions, more and more numerous though they came to be—for the demand stimulated the supply—could never in the very nature of things meet all the varied requirements of daily life. Further rules of law therefore had to be devised in some way by the jurists. At first they did this on the general basis of what they thought was right and proper, as is well illustrated by the certainly apocryphal story of the conversation between Mohammed and one (Mu'adh) whom he was sending as a judge to the Yemen. "On what," Mohammed is said to have asked, "will you base your judgments?" "On the Book of God," Mu'adh replied. "But supposing there is nothing therein to help you?" "Then," said Mu'adh, "I will judge by the Sunna of the Prophet." "But supposing

<hr>

[13] Cf. *Origins*, 58 ff.; *Law in the Middle East*, p. 42.

there is nothing there, either, to help you?" "Then I will follow my own opinion," Mu'adh is supposed to have replied; and Mohammed is said to have thanked the Almighty that He had vouchsafed him such a worthy emissary.

It was not very long, however, before the view came to prevail that this juristic opinion (*ra'y*) was at once too subjective and too fallible a basis on which to found a law which was divinely authoritative. It was too subjective; and so the jurist's general sense of what was the right rule came to be largely confined to an application of strict rules of analogy (*qiyas*), by which a rule contained in the Koran or Sunna could be extended to some similar, but not identical, situation. But it was also too fallible, for it was recognized that even in the application of rules of analogy an individual jurist might err. So the opinion gained ground among the Sunnis—partly, it seems, by way of reaction to the infallible Imam, or leader, whom the "heterodox" Shi'is claimed—that although individuals might err, the great jurists, collectively, could not; so the consensus of the jurists (or, as it is sometimes put, of the Muslim community) came to be regarded as yet another manifestation of the divine voice.

It was thus that in the classical view of Islamic jurisprudence the Shari'a was held to be based on the Koran, the Sunna, and the consensus, together with analogical deductions from these. Certain subsidiary sources are also commonly mentioned in this connection, but need not detain us now. It is, however, worthy of passing note that an enormous proportion of the law rests in fact on these last two sources (consensus and analogy), and that there is a sense in which the consensus has proved in history the most important source of all—for even the Koran stood in need of interpretation, while the traditions stood in need of authentication as well; and it was the consensus alone which in the final analysis was in a position to give an authoritative ruling.

There are three further points I want to emphasize. First, that in the early days any adequately qualified jurist was regarded as having the faculty of *ijtihad*, that is, the right to go back to the original sources and interpret them for himself. But with the passage of the years, the crystallization of the different schools of law and the progressive enunciation of the doctrine, this faculty was held to have fallen into abeyance; and, since about the end of the third century of the Hijra, all jurists have been regarded as mere *muqallids*, that is, those whose duty it is to accept the opinions of their great predecessors without the exercise of private judgment. It is true that many authorities allow that even a *muqallid* may, in the exigencies of private life, pick and choose between the different opinions of his great predecessors; but it was generally asserted that the judge and the jurisconsult had no such liberty in their public capacity, but must follow the dominant opinion in their particular school in every detail. It was thus that until recently Sunni Islam had become largely moribund. The law was still the principal discipline for study; but this study showed itself in the production of commentaries, glosses, more commentaries and more glosses—most of them representing a substantial repetition of what had gone before. There was indeed a certain development, particularly in the books of *Fatawa* or legal decisions, but it was very slow; and it was the dominant opinion that came to prevail in each of the schools, on this point or that, which constituted the authoritative criterion.

Second, what of these schools of law to which I have made a number of references? Suffice it to say that in the early days the jurists tended to draw together on a regional basis, as we find in Iraq, Medina, Syria, and elsewhere. At a somewhat later date they came to group themselves around some dominant figure, such as Shafi'i; whereupon even the regional groupings began to call themselves by the name of one of their leading jurists. Eventually four schools not only established themselves but survived in Sunni Islam (the Hanafis, Malikis, Shafi'is, and Hanbalis); and these, although they differ from each other on innumerable points, mutually recognize each other's orthodoxy. In addition there are a number of "heterodox" schools; there are records of schools that once existed but have not survived; and there are a multitude of variant opinions either attributed to early jurists before the schools crystallized or championed by more independent thinkers throughout the long history of Islam.

Third, it is noteworthy that although in theory all parts of the divine law rest equally on revelation, in practice a certain distinction can in fact be made. It is the personal and family law that, together with rules of ritual and religious observance, has always been regarded as the very heart of the Shari'a. The public law, on the other hand, although in theory equally based on divine authority, has been much less meticulously observed down the centuries. I shall return to this subject later on.

This, then, was the position up till about 1850. It is against this essential background that we must view those recent reforms that will constitute the subject of the next lecture, when I shall trace the attempts which have been made during the last century or so to bring the law more into line with the facts of modern life, and when I shall consider the fascinating problem of how a theoretically immutable law can in fact be amended in practice.

. 2 .

ISLAMIC LAW AND MODERN LIFE: RECONCILIATION IN THE MIDDLE EAST

In the first lecture we saw that to the Muslim the Shari'a is more than a religious law, it is a divine law—and, as such, essentially immutable. Further, it covers every sphere of life and every field of law. In theory, therefore, it can brook no rival, but is virtually monolithic in its claims. When, however, we turn to the heart of the Muslim world —the Arab countries of the Near and Middle East—we find that in most of them enormous changes have been effected during the last century or so in both the system of courts and the law which they apply. These I shall now discuss.

It has been aptly remarked that law is "the distilled essence of the civilization of a people,"[1] and that it reflects that people's soul more clearly than any other organism.[2] This means that the law—in its general features at least— must be of vital interest not only to the lawyer but to

[1] A. S. Diamond, *Evolution of Law and Order* (London, 1949), p. 303.

[2] D. Hughes Parry, *Haldane Memorial Lecture*, 1951, p. 3.

every student of a civilization, people, or area, whatever his particular angle of approach may be. But if this statement is true in general terms, it is beyond question particularly applicable to the Muslim world, where it has been justly noted that the sacred law has represented both the master science and the most effective agent in molding the social order and community life of Muslim peoples, and that it has held the social fabric of Islam compact and secure through all the fluctuations of political fortune.[3]

Yet the most cursory glance at the law that prevails in the Middle East today reveals the fact that it is a hotch-potch, part Islamic and indigenous and part secular and Western. So it might, of course, be argued that it is only the first element—the part of the law that is still Islamic and indigenous—that can be regarded as in any real way reflecting the soul of the peoples concerned. This was indeed probably the case at the time when "Western" law was first introduced in these countries. But it is not so, I suggest, any longer. On the contrary, it seems to me that this amalgam of the ancient and modern, the indigenous and the Western, the Islamic and the secular, provides a vivid and, in the main, faithful picture of the whole background, and even mentality, of these peoples today.

One further point by way of general introduction. I believe that it is fair to say, first, that the measures of reform in the law as a whole, which have been introduced in most of these countries over the past century, provide both a mirror and a gauge of their social progress and even national development; and, second, that the measures of reform in that part of the law that is still specifically Islamic,

[3] Cf. H. A. R. Gibb *Mohammedanism* (London, 1953), pp. 9–11.

which have been introduced in country after country
over the last forty years, constitute at one and the same
time a most significant example of modernism in Islam,
where theology and law always go hand in hand, and also
a fascinating illustration of how a theoretically immutable
law can in fact be amended in practice.

But it is imperative, I think, to approach this subject
initially from a historical perspective. So let us start from
this postulate: that up till little more than a century ago
the canon law of Islam reigned supreme, nominally at
least, throughout the entire Middle East. But this statement needs a certain amount of elucidation and a considerable degree of qualification.

In orthodox theory the life of a Muslim has always been
dominated by the twin sciences of theology and law.
Theology prescribes all that he must believe; law, all that
he must do or leave undone. And this vast structure of
theology and law was built up on the basis of divine
revelation, which was regarded as providing the only safe
criterion for either faith or practice. In the classical theory, then, the Shari'a was derived, as we have seen, from
four main sources—the Koran, the Sunna of the Prophet,
the consensus of the jurists, and analogical deductions
from these—although in historical fact pre-Islamic customary law, and the administrative practice of early Islam,
provided the raw material out of which a great part of the
Shari'a was evolved.

With the passage of time, as we have noted, orthodox
Islam resolved itself into four schools of law: the Hanafi,
Maliki, Shafi'i, and Hanbali. But the "heterodox" schools
of the Ibadis and the different subsects of the Shi'a also
survived. In addition, the teachings of extinct schools, such

as the Zahiris, are still available for consultation, as are also a multitude of dicta attributed to early jurists or advocated by individual scholars as variant (but unsuccessful) opinions within the recognized schools. There was thus a mass of material available; yet the fact remained that in each school a dominant opinion on almost every point came to prevail. Whereas, moreover, it had previously been the practice, sometimes at least, for Qadis representing each of the four Sunni schools to hold court simultaneously in the principal cities of Islam, the Ottoman authorities recognized the Hanafi school as the only official doctrine of the empire; so the most authoritative Hanafi opinion on each point became uniquely authoritative.

So much for the elucidation of the postulate that up till little more than a century ago the canon law of Islam reigned supreme, nominally at least, throughout the entire Middle East. But this statement also stands in need of a measure of qualification. For although, as we have seen, the Shari'a was in theory all-inclusive, it was never in fact applied in its purity and entirety throughout every sphere of life. This was particularly true of public law, or criminal, administrative, and constitutional law; for the rules of evidence and procedure laid down in the Shari'a were so rigid and exacting that the executive was seldom, if ever, willing to leave the maintenance of public order exclusively to the Qadis and their courts (committed as they were to the Shari'a, officially at least, in every particular). It was also true, in a somewhat different way, of the field of commercial law; for here the doctrinaire prohibition of "usury" and of speculative contracts made demands that the merchants found intolerably severe in the life of the markets. As a result, various rival jurisdictions began to appear at a very early date—such as the Court of Complaints, the police, and the inspector of markets, or such as informal courts of mercantile arbitration. But however this might be, the Shari'a remained nominally supreme in every sphere of law; there was no rival code, and such other jurisdictions as existed were not officially recognized as rivals. And the Shari'a, as we have seen, had become largely moribund.

It is against this background that the political and cultural incursions of the West, and the subsequent Turkish and Arab awakenings, must be viewed. It is eminently understandable, then, that the first and basic reform should have taken the form of the establishment of specifically secular courts alongside the Shari'a courts, and the introduction of codes of law for these courts to apply.

It was thus that the Ottoman authorities promulgated the Commercial Code in 1850, the Penal Code in 1858, the Code of Commercial Procedure in 1861, and the Code of Maritime Commerce in 1863—all based on European (and, in particular, on French) models. Even so, this legislation was represented as additional, rather than contrary, to the Shari'a, and these early reforms coexisted with the retention of such controversial features in the Shari'a as the death penalty for apostasy, while it was only after a protracted struggle that non-Muslim witnesses became eligible to testify in any case involving Muslim litigants. Instead, moreover, of adopting a European code to cover the basic law of obligations, the Ottoman authorities decided, in the Majalla, on a compromise—for between 1869 and 1876 they compiled, in the form of a more or less modern code, principles and precepts drawn in fact from the Shari'a. More important still, from some points of view, the Tanzimat reforms saw the establishment of secular courts—both mixed, for cases involving foreigners, and nizami, for cases involving only Ottoman subjects—alongside the Shari'a courts, which were thenceforward to be confined to cases of personal status and family law (in the widest connotation of those terms).

Similarly, in Egypt, which had attained its juridical independence under the Khedive Isma'il, mixed courts were set up in 1875 and native courts in 1883, and two civil codes, together with a penal code, were promulgated for these courts to apply. These codes represented extensive adoptions of the Napoleonic legislation, although the civil codes included a number of sections drawn instead from the Shari'a. It is noteworthy, however, that a penal code may always be regarded, or at least passed off, as a mere codification of the way in which that discretionary (*ta'zir*) jurisdiction which represents the overwhelmingly greater part of Islamic criminal law is to be exercised by the courts; and it was in fact provided in the Egyptian code that no Muslim should be executed until the Mufti had been consulted as to whether the death penalty was applicable in such circumstance under the Shari'a, while it was also expressly stated that this code must not be held to nullify any private right sanctioned thereby. But however that may be, it is clear that from the beginning of the last quarter of the nineteenth century the Shari'a courts in Egypt, as throughout the rest of the Ottoman Empire, were restricted to questions of personal status and family law; so the dichotomy in the courts—and, to a considerable extent, in the law they were to apply—was complete.

It might well be asked why it was that the Shari'a was

thus progressively set on one side in favor of codes derived largely from the West. Initially, it seems clear, this was far less the result of any popular demand for reform (although such demand there was, particularly among the non-Muslim subjects of the Ottoman Empire) than imposed upon the people from above, partly in the interest of administrative efficiency and national progress, and partly in order to satisfy foreign opinion. But as time went on, the conservative opposition to these reforms was challenged by a variety of arguments put forward by the more progressive elements in the countries concerned. Some used political arguments, such as the need to follow in the path of Western progress and to convince the West of their emancipation from those points in the Shari'a that attracted the most adverse comment—such as mutilation for theft, stoning for adultery, talion for deliberate homicide or wounding, and a maximum period of gestation fixed by the Hanafis at two years, the Shafi'is at four, and by most Malikis at five. Some, instead, used economic arguments, such as dissatisfaction with the *waqf* system, which kept a large proportion of the nation's natural resources maladministered and withdrawn from commerce under the "dead hand," or with the meticulous restrictions of the law of "usury," which, if rigidly applied, would have meant the abandonment of the vast majority of fiscal operations to non-Muslims. Others, again, used legal arguments, such as the inadequacy of archaic rules of procedure and evidence, which left litigation largely at the mercy of rigid principles as to what evidence was admissible or inadmissible, rather than a common-sense approach to the weight to be accorded to this testimony or that; or such as the need for a code that could be consulted and, to some extent at least, understood by any educated person. And yet others used social arguments, such as the need for reforms in the law of marriage and divorce that were blocked by an immutable law, and such as the imperative need for society and the law which governs it to progress together.

Thus to displace the Shari'a almost in its entirety from such a wide range of subjects as the commercial law, the criminal law, and much of the civil law, and to substitute in its place codes of largely Western inspiration, might appear to the Western mind the most drastic expedient possible. But it must be emphasized that to many Muslims of the more conservative type, particularly at this period, it seemed much less drastic than any attempt to amend the Shari'a. For they preferred to preserve its sacred precepts intact, as the ideal law for the golden age—even if this involved largely replacing it in practice in favor of a secular code forced upon them by the exigencies of modern life— rather than to permit any profane meddling with its immutable provisions.

It is precisely in this context that the Majalla assumes such vital significance. Here was an authoritative codification for the first time in history of rules derived from the Shari'a—and a codification based not exclusively on the dominant Hanafi opinion regarding every point, but rather on an eclectic selection of provisions that had received recognition of some sort in the Hanafi school (even though some of them had originated in fact elsewhere). This was an innovation of outstanding importance, which found its juristic justification in the broad principle that the ruler has the right both to define and to confine the jurisdiction of his courts. This principle, moreover, was given two major applications: first, that whereas the courts —by contrast, as we have seen, with the individual Muslim—were ordinarily considered to be bound by the most authoritative Hanafi opinion in every particular, they could be directed to substitute some variant view, provided it had adequate authority, in those particulars which the ruler so specified in the public interests; and second, that the ruler might in those same interests totally exclude certain causes in specified circumstances from the competence of his courts, and thus deny any judicial enforcement of certain claims that might be justified (and otherwise enforced) under the Shari'a. But it must be emphasized that up till 1915 these principles of reform had been confined to the law of obligations, as codified in the Majalla; had scarcely been extended to any opinions which could claim no Hanafi support; and had in no case been applied to that stronghold of the pure Shari'a, the personal and family law.

Let us briefly review the position up till 1915. Before that date the commercial and penal law (which are always, perhaps, the parts of the law of primary importance to foreigners) had been largely Westernized, both in regard to the substantive law and the courts which applied it. The same was also true of the courts which applied the basic law of contract and tort, but here the substantive law, although largely Westernized in Egypt, had been modernized in form rather than Westernized in substance throughout the rest of the Ottoman Empire. It was only the family law, in its widest connotation, that was still applied in the old courts, from the old books, in the old way, and by the old personnel. And it is the family law that, though of less immediate importance to the foreigner, provides the most faithful mirror of social change and also—in Islam—the outstanding example of how a nominally immutable law can be modified in practice.

It was the miserable lot of Muslim wives that first prompted, and indeed forced, the extension of the principles of reform to the sacred sphere of the family law. For a Muslim wife, according to the most authoritative Hanafi opinion, had no right to a judicial dissolution of her marriage even if deserted by her husband for year after year, or if she found herself married, without her knowledge, to a man afflicted with some such disease of body or mind as leprosy or insanity. This was an intolerable position, which was remedied in 1915 by two imperial edicts—the one, based officially on Hanbali doctrine (although the Maliki teaching might equally have been quoted in support), granting relief to deserted wives, and the other, based on a variant opinion within the Hanafi school (although supported this time by the dominant doctrine of each of the other Sunni schools), allowing a judicial dissolution of marriage at the behest of wives whose husbands proved to be afflicted with some such disease as to make married life dangerous. The dike once breached, progress was rapid, and in 1917 the Ottoman Law of Family Rights was promulgated. This was a fairly complete codification of the personal and family law, with the exception of the law of testate and intestate succession; it derived its provisions not only from Hanafi doctrine, but from a selection of rules taken from the four Sunni schools; it included a number of administrative regulations, breach of which was punishable under the criminal law; and it comprised special sections for Jews and Christians, for it was designed to unify jurisdiction before the national courts. And while this law proved extremely short-lived in Turkey, it survived—in so far as Muslims alone were concerned—much longer in Syria and Jordan (with some modifications in the latter), and is still applied today in Lebanon and Israel. It was never applied in Iraq, which had been liberated by the Allies before its promulgation in Istanbul; but the two imperial edicts of 1915 had, of course, already been applied in that territory.

Meanwhile the reformers were equally, or even more, active in Egypt, where Qasim Amin published his book *The Liberation of Woman* around the turn of the century and where the dominant figure of Mohammed 'Abduh was in the forefront of the champions of progress. There was, however, much opposition; and it was not until a committee composed both of ulema and practicing lawyers was set up in 1915, under the chairmanship of Mustafa'l-Maraghi, the then Shaykh of the Azhar (who had already established his popularity in that ancient university by the introduction of a number of notable reforms), that progress was made. Even so, World War I intervened; and it was not until 1920 and 1929 that reforms were actually promulgated in the law of marriage and divorce, while 1923 saw a distinct advance in regard to child-marriage.[4]

It is also noteworthy—and little known—that many of these early (and subsequent) Egyptian reforms were introduced in the then Anglo-Egyptian Sudan even before they were promulgated in Egypt. The legislative basis for this was a provision to the effect that the Shari'a courts in that

[4] It is, however, noteworthy that reforms in the law of procedure and evidence followed in the Shari'a courts were made in Egypt, at intervals, from just before the end of the previous century.

country must always follow the dominant opinion of the Hanafi school except in those particulars in which the Grand Qadi, with the agreement of the government, had issued a judicial circular specifying some variant opinion that was to be applied in its stead.[5] At this time, moreover, the Grand Qadi was always an Egyptian jurist, and Mustafa'l-Maraghi had himself served in this capacity. It is not altogether surprising, therefore, that some of the reforms under debate in Egypt were tried out initially in the Sudan, while others were adopted there subsequent to their promulgation in Egypt.

If we compare these early Egyptian reforms with the Ottoman Law of Family Rights, it is immediately obvious that the Egyptian legislation was much more fragmentary, as well as slightly later, than the Ottoman, but that it was also a great deal more radical. These reforms found their juristic basis not only in some variant Hanafi view or in the dominant doctrine of one of the other Sunni schools, but sometimes also in opinions attributed to early Muslim jurists or to extinct schools, sometimes in the doctrine of heterodox schools (although this was usually shrouded in references to certain early Sunni commentators), sometimes in that combination, in a single whole, of elements from two or more different schools or jurists which is termed *talfiq,* and sometimes in what can be regarded only as a new interpretation of the original sources (although this again was seldom acknowledged openly).

I shall not pause to describe these reforms in any detail now, although I believe them to be of outstanding interest, because they were almost exclusively concerned

[5] For details see my article, "Recent Developments in Shari'a Law in the Sudan," *Sudan Notes and Records,* XXI (1950).

with the law of marriage and divorce, which is the subject of the next lecture. Suffice it to say that they consisted in the main in provisions designed to give ill-used wives the right to a judicial divorce, in measures calculated to discourage child-marriage, and in an attempt to impose certain restrictions on the ridiculously wide scope of validity attributed to formulas of divorce pronounced by Muslim husbands. A single example of certain other, and more heterogeneous, provisions may, however, be of interest; for the ancient views regarding the maximum period of gestation were neatly side-stepped by the device of forbidding the courts to entertain any claim—whether for maintenance, paternity, or inheritance—based on a period of gestation that was alleged to have lasted more than a solar year.[6]

Such in the main were the Egyptian reforms up till 1929. It was some years before a further step was taken—except for a code of procedure promulgated in 1931. But in 1936 a committee was set up to prepare a complete codification of the law of personal status; and this committee was in fact responsible for drafting the Law of Inheritance, 1943, the Law of the Rules of Waqf, 1946, and the Law of Testamentary Dispositions, 1946. Each of these represented a comparatively complete codification of the relevant law, and thus largely relieved the courts of the necessity for referring to the ancient texts. In addition, each (and particularly the last two) effected some

[6] For details see my articles, "Recent Developments in Shari'a Law" I-V, in successive numbers of *The Muslim World*, XL (1950)–XLI (1951); and "The Problem of Divorce in the Shari'a Law of Islam," in *Journal of the Royal Central Asian Society*, XXXVII (1950), 169–85.

outstanding reforms. Since, however, my fourth lecture is to be devoted to the Islamic law of inheritance, I shall content myself here with observing that the Law of the Rules of Waqf provided—entirely contrary to precedent—that any future *waqf* would in all cases (except a mosque or cemetery) remain revocable by its founder during his lifetime; that any charitable *waqf* (except one in support of a mosque) might in future be either permanent or temporary in character; and that no family *waqf* must ever in future be designed to last more than sixty years, or two series of beneficiaries, after its founder's death.[7]

This, then, is the present position in Egypt in regard to the reform of that part of the law that is still specifically Islamic—except, that is, for four additional points. First, that in 1947 the Law of the Hisbiya Courts was promulgated, to come into force in the next year, as a comprehensive codification of the law of legal capacity, of the guardianship of property, and of the representation of absent persons, and so forth—matters that now fall within the competence of these new Hisbiya courts. Second, that in 1952 the present revolutionary regime decreed the abolition of private or family *waqfs,* and the progressive liquidation of existing ones. Third, that the same regime took the bold decision of abolishing, from 1956, both the Shari'a courts and the courts of the non-Muslim communities—a decision to which I shall return later on. Finally, that it is understood that a comprehensive code of personal and family law is now in draft in Egypt, ready for promulgation; but it seems distinctly doubtful whether

[7] For details see my articles, "Recent Developments in Shari'a Law" VI, VII and IX, in *The Muslim World,* XLII (1952).

this draft will ever be enacted as such, since it is apparently considerably more conservative in tenor than the Syrian Law of Personal Status, 1953—and it would appear unlikely that this opportunity to make an attempt to unify the law of personal status throughout the United Arab Republic will be allowed to go by default.

But another and parallel development has also taken place in Egypt in regard to the more general law, for in 1948 a new civil code was enacted, to come into effect in 1949 at the time of the abolition of the mixed courts. This code was primarily based on the two existing codes; but such emphasis was placed on the fact that it was to be enriched—first from the case law of the Egyptian courts, second from comparative legislation on the widest basis, and third from the Islamic law—that this might easily be forgotten. The emphasis placed on these sources of enrichment echoes, indeed, a growing antipathy to any "slavish adoption" of foreign legislation; instead, the legislators were urged to make an intelligent choice between the best provisions in all contemporary codes and, above all, to make a more extensive use of their own cultural heritage. Not a few voices maintained, in fact, that a code of civil law adequate to all the demands of modern life could be derived from the principles of the Shari'a alone; but it is noteworthy that in sober reality some three-quarters or five-sixths of the new code comes directly from its predecessors, and that, in spite of all the propaganda about the riches of the Shari'a, the code of 1949 reveals little more direct borrowing therefrom than those of 1875 and 1883— although former borrowings from that source were retained, principles recognized therein were allegedly sometimes made the criterion as to whether the "Latin" or "Germanic" approach was preferred, and Article I provides that, in default of any relevant provision in the code, the court shall be guided by "customary law, the principles of Islamic law, or the principles of natural justice." Not only so, but we find that the chief architect of the code, 'Abd al-Razzaq al-Sanhuri, while claiming that he would yield to none in his devotion to the Shari'a, not only admitted that little that was new had in fact been borrowed exclusively therefrom, but added, significantly: "I assure you that we did not leave a single sound provision of the Shari'a which we could have included in this legislation without so doing. We adopted from the Shari'a all that we could, having regard to sound principles of modern legislation; and we did not fall short in this respect." [8]

But Egypt is by no means alone in such reforms, which are today sweeping through one Arab country after another. We have seen how the Egyptian reforms in family law were in fact preceded by the Ottoman Law of Family Rights; and were also preceded in some points, and followed in others, in the Sudan. But much has been taking place recently elsewhere.

In Jordan, for instance, the Majalla is still applied in civil cases—as is also the case in Israel. But in 1951 the Ottoman Law of Family Rights was replaced by the Jordanian Law of Family Rights. This ranges over the whole law of family relations other than questions of testate and intestate succession; it grafts most (though not all) the

[8] For details see my article, "The Shari'a and Civil Law (the debt owed by the new Civil Codes of Egypt and Syria to the Shari'a)," *Islamic Quarterly*, I (1954), 29–46.

Egyptian reforms onto the stem of the Ottoman Law; and it includes a few minor innovations of its own.[9]

In Syria, on the other hand, the Majalla was displaced in 1949 in favor of a new civil code which represents, for the most part, an almost verbal adoption of the code promulgated in Egypt the year before, except for the sections concerned with proof and real property. This was said to be a step along the path leading to the unification of the law in all Arab countries. In 1949, too, private or family *waqfs* were abolished in Syria, and principles laid down for the liquidation of existing ones; and in 1953 the Ottoman Law of Family Rights was replaced by the Syrian Law of Personal Status. This is indeed the most comprehensive of all such codes; it includes questions of legal capacity, guardianship, and representation, as in the Jordanian law, but also questions of testate and intestate succession, unlike the Jordanian; it incorporates two outstanding innovations in regard to the law of marriage and divorce, which I shall discuss in the next lecture; and it is applicable to all Syrians, except (as expressly provided) that it is not applicable to the Druzes in regard to certain points in which their law is radically different, and it is applicable to Christians and Jews only in regard to questions of succession, paternity, capacity, and representation. This means presumably that the Nusayris (or 'Alawis) and the Shi'is (of both the Ithna 'Ashari and Isma'ili sects) are entirely governed, officially at least, by its terms.[10]

[9] For details see my article, "Recent Developments in Shari'a Law" VIII, *The Muslim World*, XLII (1952).

[10] For details see my article, "The Syrian Law of Personal Status," *Bulletin of the School of Oriental and African Studies,* XVII (1955), 34–49.

In Tunisia the outstanding phenomenon is the Tunisian Law of Personal Status, which was brought into force on January 1, 1957. Previous to this there had been both Hanafi and Maliki Qadis in Tunis, although the people are predominantly Malikis. Now, however, this new, eclectic code is applicable to all Muslims (and has subsequently been accepted by, and applied to, the Jewish community); the courts have been unified; and all jurisdiction is now in the hands of the national courts. But the new code—which covers intestate, but not yet testate, succession—also includes several startling innovations in the law of marriage and divorce, as we shall see in the next lecture. It is significant, moreover, that President Bourguiba, in his forthright way, asserted that "ideas which were valid in the past today offend the human spirit—such as polygamy, divorce as the law now stands, and all the problems to which these give rise in modern life." Islam, he said, had liberated the spirit, and bidden men reflect on religious laws in order to adapt them to human progress. This is far removed from the voice of Islamic orthodoxy.[11]

But the most recent of all these codes is the Moroccan Code of Personal Status, 1958. The Books of Marriage and Divorce were brought into effect on January 1; the Book of Paternity on January 3; the Book of Capacity and Representation on January 7; the Book of Bequests on March 7; and the Book of Intestate Succession on April 4. This shows the urgency and determination with which the project was pursued. The code is, moreover, almost as comprehensive as the Syrian legislation, and it incorpo-

[11] For details see my article, "The Tunisian Law of Personal Status," *The International and Comparative Law Quarterly,* VII (1958), 262–79.

rates a number of reforms of outstanding interest, especially in the sphere of marriage and divorce. In general terms these may be said to be more progressive than the Syrian reforms, but more conservative than the Tunisian innovations.[12]

What, it may be asked, of Lebanon, Libya, and Iraq? In Lebanon, as has been remarked already, the Ottoman Law of Family Rights is still in force, and is applied to Shi'is "as far as it is not contrary to their personal law." But in 1947 the Lebanese Law of Family Waqfs was promulgated. This was based very largely on the corresponding sections of the Egyptian Law of the Rules of Waqf, 1946, and, like its Egyptian model, severely limited the duration of all family *waqfs*. In 1948, moreover, the Law of Personal Status for the Druze Community was enacted;[13] but a general Law of Inheritance, which was in draft at the end of 1949, was never promulgated, chiefly because of opposition from Muslim quarters. In the sphere of civil law, on the other hand, what remained of the Majalla was finally displaced in 1932 by the Law of Obligations and Contracts, a piece of legislation resting firmly on French foundations.

In Libya the Egyptian Civil Code has been adopted almost verbatim. The Criminal Code, on the other hand, presents the curious phenomenon of deriving its sections on general principles from Egypt and its sections on specific crimes from Italy, a phenomenon which must, of course, find its explanation on historical grounds. The

[12] For details see my article, "Reforms in Family Law in Morocco," *Journal of African Law*, II (1958), 146–59.

[13] For details see my article, "The Personal Law of the Druze Community," *Die Welt des Islams*, N.S., II (1952), 1–9, 83–94.

Libyans are also understood to be currently committed to a codification of their personal and family law along the lines we have seen elsewhere; and they are said to incline toward the Syrian model, but with a natural predilection for Maliki principles.

In Iraq there has hitherto been no reform in the personal law since the two imperial decrees of 1915. A comprehensive Code of Personal Status has indeed been in draft since before 1949; but this code—chiefly remarkable perhaps for the fact that it includes different provisions in many of its articles for Sunnis and for Ja'faris—has not yet been promulgated because of the opposition it aroused (mainly, it is said, on the part of the Ja'fari leaders).[14] In 1951, on the other hand, a new civil code was brought into operation. This had been drawn up by a committee in which 'Abd al-Razzaq al-Sanhuri (the Egyptian) had again taken the leading part; but it is considerably more Islamic than the Egyptian code, in spite of the remarks Sanhuri made with regard to the Egyptian legislation. The most probable explanation of this apparent inconsistency is, of course, that in Iraq the Majalla had remained in force right up till the promulgation of the new code—which represents in fact a sort of amalgam between the Majalla and the Egyptian legislation—whereas Egypt had already experienced some seventy years of predominantly French law. All the same, it is noteworthy that emphasis is placed, in the explanatory memorandum that accompanied this code, on the fact that it represented an initial attempt to draw up an Arab civil code on which

[14] For details see my article, "A Draft Code of Personal Law for 'Iraq," *Bulletin of the School of Oriental and African Studies,* XV (1953), 43–60.

all the Arab countries could unite; a code, it was said, that would represent the golden mean between the excessive Westernization of some of these countries and the exaggerated conservatism of others. And it was also stated that further enlightened study of the Shari'a would no doubt reveal yet further riches that could be exploited to this end.

This summary brings us more or less up to date in the Arab countries, except for the Arabian Peninsula itself. In Saudi Arabia, the Yemen, and elsewhere in the peninsula the Shari'a still—nominally at least—reigns supreme. Yet even in Saudi Arabia royal decrees are today assuming an ever-increasing importance. And it is noteworthy that even in Mukalla and Shihr, in the Eastern Aden Protectorate, reforms based on the juristic foundations I have discussed in this lecture have been introduced on more than one occasion.[15] But we must leave any further consideration of Arabia—and indeed of Turkey, where the Shari'a has been completely excluded from the jurisdiction of the courts—for the last lecture of this series.

[15] For details see my book, *Islamic Law in Africa* (London, 1954), pp. 16 ff.

. 3 .

THE ISLAMIC LAW OF
MARRIAGE AND DIVORCE

In the first lecture we saw that Islamic law is a transcendental law that has a validity of its own quite distinct from that of any human legislature or judiciary; for it challenges the obedience of ruler and subject, judge and litigant, councilor and citizen alike. We saw indeed that it is regarded as a divine law, firmly founded on a revelation of eternal validity—and so in theory as virtually immutable in its provisions. And we saw too that it covers every aspect of life and every field of human behavior, with no distinction whatever, in theory, between the religious and the secular, between church and state.

In the second lecture we turned from the theory of the divine law to the actual position in the Middle East today. We reviewed the way in which the Shari'a was first substantially put on one side, in regard to most aspects of life, in favor of codes of predominantly Western inspiration, and then the way in which reforms were effected, by a series of ingenious devices, even within the sacred sphere of the law of family relations.

Now for the next two lectures we turn to two specific branches of Islamic law—the Islamic law of marriage and divorce and the Islamic law of inheritance—to examine these in rather more detail.

But the question might well be asked: Why these, rather than, let us say, commercial or company law? Would not the latter be much more interesting and important for an American? The answer would be that commercial and company law in these countries today—except, in general, in Arabia itself—is not really Islamic but Western. So, however important that law may be in practice to those who trade in the area, it is not very interesting in the context of these lectures.

Instead, I have chosen the law of marriage and divorce for our consideration, for four very good reasons:

First, because, as we have seen, it is the family law that has always represented the very heart of the Shari'a, for it is this part of the law that is regarded by Muslims as entering into the very warp and woof of their religion.

Second, because, by the same token, it is the family law that has been basic to Islamic society down the centuries.

Third, because it is, generally speaking, in the law of the family alone that the Shari'a is still applied to some four hundred million Muslims, for it is virtually only in the Arabian Peninsula, Afghanistan, and Northern Nigeria that the Shari'a is applied today, as such, outside the sphere of family relations and personal status.

Fourth, because it is precisely in regard to the law of marriage and divorce that the battle is joined today between the forces of conservatism and progress in the Muslim world, and the vicissitudes of that battle provide, as we have seen, a gauge of social progress, a mirror of the advance of modernism in Islam, and an illustration of how a nominally immutable law can be changed in practice.

Let us start then with a summary statement of Islamic law in these matters. A Muslim woman is bound to monogamy, while a Muslim man may have as many as four wives at once, but no more. In addition, the Ithna 'Ashari branch of the Shi'a, alone, allows him any number of temporary marriages, or "marriages of enjoyment," while all schools allow a man to indulge rights of concubinage with his own female slaves. Any sexual intercourse outside these limits[1] constitutes *zina,* or illicit sex relations, for which the punishment is death by stoning in the case of an offender who has ever consummated a lawful marriage, and one hundred lashes in the case of others. But these penalties can seldom be properly imposed because of the exceedingly exacting standard of proof required, and the principle that such punishments are averted by any circumstance of doubt—besides the fact that Islamic criminal law has today only a very limited application. In addition, a Muslim husband may repudiate his wife or wives at any time and at his unilateral discretion.

So much for a very general summary. It is essential, however, first to consider this against its historical background and then to elaborate it in greater detail.

In pre-Islamic Arabia, it seems, there were several types of marriage, ranging probably from the patrilineal and patrilocal to the matrilineal and matrilocal, and including the so-called "marriage of temporary enjoyment." The most respectable form, however, was a patrilineal marriage in which the groom paid a dower for, or to, his bride.

---

[1] Or rather, outside some semblance of such relationships.

This had developed, no doubt, out of the widespread custom of paying bride-wealth to the tribe or family of the wife in consideration for the loss of her reproductive capacity and as a stabilization both of the union and of the relations between the two families; but it would seem that even before the advent of Islam the dower had come to be regarded in Arabia as properly belonging to the bride herself. In any case this is a characteristic of the Islamic law of marriage, however much it is still disregarded in practice in some quarters. Muslim jurists often in fact employ the simile of sale, and regard the dower as consideration for marital rights—a consideration that constitutes an essential element in every Muslim marriage. Nor is this dower repayable on divorce, in Islamic law, once the marriage has been consummated, even where the wife is primarily at fault, except by her own voluntary agreement.

In pre-Islamic Arabia, moreover, there was no limit to the number of wives a man might acquire, nor, it seems, to his unfettered discretion in repudiating them. But when we are told that the wives themselves had no means of escape from an odious union, we may well feel somewhat skeptical.

It is against this background that we must view the two major innovations effected by the advent of Islam:

First, polygyny was limited to a maximum of four wives at a time, according to the classical interpretation of what is often termed the "Verse of Polygamy" in the Koran. Even so, indulgence in polygamy at all was made conditional on a man's confidence that he could treat a plurality of wives impartially, and also (on one interpretation of the Arabic) on his ability to support existing dependents and assume, in addition, further responsibilities; but these conditions were regarded as resting on the sanctions of religion, not as enforceable by the courts.

Second, divorce, although permitted, was stated (in a tradition attributed to the Prophet) to be the most hateful to God of all permitted things. Its rigors were therefore mitigated somewhat by the introduction of the *'idda* period, during which a divorced (or indeed widowed) woman was precluded from remarriage; for this was designed not only to avoid doubt as to the paternity of children but also to give the husband an opportunity to reconsider any hasty action and revoke the divorce at any time before the *'idda* ended.

It seems, however, that this right was soon abused by husbands who wanted to force their wives into providing a financial consideration (e.g., return of dower) for their release, and who therefore revoked their repudiations just before the end of the *'idda* only to repudiate their wives once more, and thus keep them in an almost continual state of neither being properly married nor free. So a revelation was promulgated limiting such revocations of a repudiation to two, after which any further repudiation would be final. It appears, however, that a woman whose first marriage had ended in divorce, and who had subsequently been married to another man, asked Mohammed if she might not now, as an older and wiser woman, remarry her first husband; and that this was the origin of the rule that remarriage is permissible, even after a third (or triple) repudiation, provided that the divorced wife has in the meantime consummated a marriage with another man. It was this rule that gave rise, in the hands of the jurists, to a number of unsavory devices designed to enable a man who had repudiated his wife three times in a fit of temper to marry her once more.

Another unfortunate development in the law largely nullified one of the purposes for which the 'idda period had been instituted, namely, to provide an opportunity for second thoughts; for the custom grew up of husbands pronouncing three repudiations at one and the same time, and thus precluding themselves not only from an opportunity to revoke their repudiation, but even from the possibility of remarrying the divorced wife, except by means of one of these unsavory devices.

It is time, however, to examine the law of marriage in considerable more detail. In Islamic law marriage is emphatically not considered to be a sacrament but rests entirely on a contractual basis. Its essential constituents are declaration and acceptance, and no religious ceremony, however customary, is legally necessary. But contemporary Muslim jurists, after treating these *arkan,* or essential constituents, commonly treat the *shurut,* or conditions for a valid marriage, under five different headings.

First, they discuss conditions governing the conclusion of the contract of marriage. These are that the declaration and acceptance must agree together, must be pronounced at the same "meeting" of the parties, must be in terms effecting an immediate union, and must issue from persons legally competent to conclude such a contract.

Here the only point that need detain us, I think, is the fact that all schools allow a marriage guardian to contract a marriage in respect of his minor ward. The Malikis, Shafi'is, and Hanbalis, moreover, insist that even an adult woman must be contracted in marriage by her guardian (or in some cases by the court acting in his place). The

Hanafis, on the other hand, consider that an adult woman may contract herself in marriage provided she chooses a husband who is her "equal" in respect of family, trade, religion, and so forth; that only minors may be given in marriage without their consent; and that even minors have an option of repudiating such a marriage when they reach majority in all cases in which the guardian who acted for them was other than father or grandfather.[2] The other Sunni schools exclude marriage by compulsion by any except the father or father's father (or, in the case of the Malikis, the father or his executor); but they extend such compulsion, in respect of virgin daughters, far beyond majority.

The introduction of reforms designed to eliminate child-marriage represents a matter of considerable delicacy to the pious Muslim, since Mohammed himself married one of his wives at an exceedingly early age. All the same, the reformers have made much progress in this matter, most of which will be discussed later. It is significant, however, that the explanatory memorandum issued with the Ottoman Law of Family Rights, 1917, included an impassioned description of the evils—to husband, wife, children, and society—of premature marriage, while the two most recent codes, those of Tunisia and Morocco, represent a complete abandonment of the Maliki law regarding marriage by compulsion previously applicable in those countries. The Tunisian Code, in fact, empowers a girl who has reached

[2] And the Ithna 'Ashari Shi'is agree with the Hanafis that an adult woman may contract herself in marriage and that only minors may be given in compulsory marriage; but they confine such compulsion to the father and grandfather.

majority to dispense entirely with the intervention of her guardian, and it is only between the statutory minimum age for marriage and the age of full majority that the consent of such agnatic guardian, or the court, is required. In Morocco the intervention of the marriage guardian is still necessary; but the ancient right of the father to give his daughter in compulsory marriage has been transformed, as in Tunisia, into a means of protection for one who has reached the minimum age for marriage but not that of full majority, and no marriage may validly be contracted in either country without the consent of the parties themselves (except only that in Morocco the court may give a girl whose morals are in jeopardy in marriage to a suitable suitor and protector).[3]

Second, Muslim writers discuss conditions governing the validity of a contract so concluded, for even where the contract itself is beyond reproach, the marriage will not be valid unless these further conditions are fulfilled. Chief among these, of course, are the requirement that the parties should not be within the prohibited degrees, whether of blood relationship, marriage relationship, or (and this is distinctively Islamic) foster relationship. And it is noteworthy that even in Turkey (although not, curiously enough, in the Turkish Family [Marriage and Divorce] Laws, 1951 and 1954, in Cyprus) the bar of foster

[3] A further difference is that in Morocco a guardian may still object to the marriage of his major ward with one who is not her "equal," whereas in Tunisia no such restriction remains. For this whole subject cf. Arts. 3–10 of the Tunisian Code and Arts. 6–15 of the Moroccan Code, also my articles on these codes (as quoted above).

relationship has been inserted among the provisions of the Swiss Civil Code (as there adopted).[4]

In addition, a man is prohibited from being married, at one and the same time, to two women who would be debarred, were one of them a male, from marrying each other;[5] a woman who is already married or still observing her *'idda* of widowhood or divorce is forbidden to marry anyone else; and a man who already has four wives may not marry a fifth. A Muslim man may marry a Muslim woman or one from a revealed religion (i.e., a Christian or Jewess); but a Muslim woman may not marry any but a Muslim. A further requirement of a valid marriage in Sunni law[6] is the presence of two eligible witnesses; and this requirement is a matter of substantive law, not merely an evidentiary precaution—by contrast with the Shi'i doctrine.

It is also noteworthy that some Hanafi jurists classify marriage contracts under the three categories of valid, irregular, and void; and that they accord certain legal effects to the intermediate category. It seems better, however, to postulate that no irregular or void marriage has any validity as such in Islamic law, but that in certain circumstances the children of such unions, if consummated, will be regarded as legitimate, and the woman as both

[4] Cf. my article, "The Family Law of Turkish Cypriots," *Die Welt des Islams*, N.S.V., 3–4 (1958), 161–87.

[5] More accurately, one should notionally regard first the one woman and then the other as a male, and it is only where intermarriage would be forbidden in *both* cases that the bar of affinity is raised.

[6] All except the Malikis require such witnesses to the contract as such, while the Malikis are rather less exacting in this respect.

entitled to dower and bound to observe the *'idda*, while the bar of affinity will be raised between the parties.

Third—and this need scarcely detain us—modern textbooks discuss those conditions that make a valid contract effective. For the Hanafi jurists regarded a contract concluded by a minor who had reached the age of discrimination but not of majority as valid, but suspended on whether his guardian consents thereto: if he does, it becomes effective; if he does not, it becomes null and void. Similarly, a contract of marriage concluded by a slave is regarded as suspended on his master's consent, and a contract concluded by an unauthorized person on behalf of another as suspended on the consent of the principal party; and this would also, of course, apply to an agent who acted in any way outside his competence and authority.

Fourth, Muslim jurists discuss those conditions that determine whether a valid and effective contract of marriage is binding. For there are in fact certain circumstances in which such a contract may be revoked. Such, for instance, is the case where a minor has been given in marriage under Hanafi law by anyone other than his or her father or grandfather; for the minor then has an option of revocation on attaining puberty. Such too is the case, on one view, where an adult Hanafi woman gives herself in marriage to one who is not her "equal," for her agnatic guardian may then apply to the courts to have the couple separated. And such again is the case, according to some jurists, where one party to a marriage finds that the other was afflicted at the time of the contract with some such physical defect or sickness as to prevent consummation of the union or make it dangerous for them to live together, or even where the other party is subsequently afflicted with some foul or dangerous disease.

Finally, modern jurists discuss those conditions that govern the registration of a contract of marriage. This represents, of course, an innovation for which the classical texts provide no parallel. Nevertheless, it has now assumed a major importance, for it enshrines the principal method of reform. Sometimes, for instance, it is used as a basis for the denial of all judicial relief to those who do not fulfill the specified conditions—as in Egypt, where this device has been used to discourage child-marriage by the simple expedient of forbidding the registration of any marriages in which the groom has not reached eighteen and the bride sixteen, and precluding the courts from entertaining any disputed claim of marriage which has not been so registered.[7] In every code since the Ottoman Law of Family Rights, moreover, minimum ages for marriage have been prescribed,[8] sometimes absolutely and sometimes with a certain discretion vested in the courts; in most of these codes provision is made for all such contracts to be properly registered by competent officials; any infraction of these rules incurs a penal sanction; and no unregistered marriage is recognized by the courts, at least unless or until pregnancy becomes apparent.

And precisely the same method has been used in the attempts that have been made to limit—or even prohibit—

[7] Law No. 56 of 1923, with Art. 99 of Law No. 78 of 1931.

[8] Cf. Ottoman Law of Family Rights, 1917, Arts. 4–7, 52; Jordanian Law of Family Rights, 1951, Arts. 4–5; Syrian Law of Personal Status, 1953, Arts. 15–20; Tunisian Code of Personal Status, 1957, Arts. 5–6; Moroccan Code of Personal Status, 1958, Arts. 6–9, 12.

polygamy. As long ago as the early years of this century Shaykh Mohammed 'Abduh had proposed that a man who already had one wife should be forbidden to marry another unless the courts were satisfied that he would be able to keep the two conditions for polygamy—on al-Shafi'i's view —enunciated in the Koran, namely, an equal distribution of his favors and a competence to meet all his financial obligations. Legislation to this effect was even accepted by the Egyptian Cabinet in 1927, only to be vetoed by King Fuad. No further action was then taken on this subject in any Arab country until 1953, when the Syrian Law of Personal Status provided that "the Court may withhold permission for a man who is already married to marry a second wife where it is established that he is not in a position to support them both."[9] This was mild, however, by comparison with the Tunisian Law of Personal Status, 1957, which tersely enacted that "polygamy is prohibited"[10]—a prohibition which is said to find its juristic justification in the other Koranic provision that a man should confine himself to one wife unless confident that he is capable of treating a plurality of wives with equal justice, and the assertion that both experience and revelation have made it clear that such impartiality is in fact unattainable. It is only fair to add, however, that the older jurists had urged, reasonably enough, that the Koran must not lightly be regarded as contradicting itself; and that the equal justice demanded by the "Verse of Polygamy" must therefore be interpreted in terms of those favors over which a husband has control, not the instinctive inclinations of his heart.

[9] Art. 17.
[10] Art. 18.

The Moroccan Code of Personal Status, 1958, is considerably less drastic than the Tunisian Law in this matter, for it has contented itself with enunciating the principle that "if any injustice is to be feared between co-wives, polygamy is not permitted," and with providing that a wife whose husband concludes a second marriage may always (even where she has made no such stipulation or condition in her marriage contract) "refer her case to the court to consider any injury which may have been caused to her."[11]

It is, moreover, under this same heading of conditions governing the registration of contracts of marriage that we should notice an interesting attempt to tackle the problem of marriages in which there is too wide a disparity between the ages of the parties. Such unions have been all too common in the past; but first the Jordanian Law of Family Rights, 1951, then the Syrian Law of Personal Status, 1953, and now the Moroccan Law of Personal Status, 1958, have provided safeguards against any such union being imposed against her interests on the younger party.[12]

One further point with regard to the Islamic law of marriage should, I think, be mentioned, both for its intrinsic interest and its use by the reformers, namely, the debate as to the validity of conditions or stipulations inserted in contracts of marriage. Here the classical doctrine of the majority of jurists divided such stipulations into three categories: those that merely reinforced some normal legal effect of marriage (e.g., stipulations regarding the payment of dower), which were regarded as valid and en-

[11] Art. 30.
[12] Arts. 6, 19, 15 respectively.

forceable; those that were so radically contrary to the nature of marriage (e.g., stipulations limiting the duration of the union) as to vitiate the contract as such; and those that might be regarded as attempts to vary the normal legal effects of marriage (e.g., stipulations that the husband should not prevent his wife from practicing her profession, and should not marry any additional wives). It was this last category that led to controversy and injustice; for all schools other than the Hanbalis held that such stipulations were null and void, while the marriage itself was valid and binding—on the grounds that the legal effects of marriage had been prescribed by the Lawgiver and were not open to variation at the discretion of the parties. It was only the Hanbalis who resisted this reasoning, insisting that although the Shari'a permitted polygamy it did not enjoin it, and although it permitted a man to forbid his wife to go out of his house (except for certain specified purposes) it did not command him to do so; so a husband who undertook not to exercise these rights must be held to his undertakings, at least to the extent that, should he nevertheless marry another wife, his first wife would be entitled to a judicial annulment of her marriage. This Hanbali doctrine was included in the Ottoman Law of Family Rights, and reappears in the Jordanian, Syrian, and Moroccan legislation.[13]

But this brings me to the whole subject of the Islamic law of divorce, a subject which I must deal with as briefly as possible.

There can, I think, be no doubt whatever that it is the Islamic law of divorce—not polygamy—which is the major

[13] Art. 38. Cf. Art. 21 of the Jordanian Law of 1951; Art. 14 of the Syrian Law of 1953; and Art. 31 of the Moroccan Code of 1958.

cause of suffering to Muslim women. It is true that there are parts of the Muslim world where divorce is commendably rare; but elsewhere it is appallingly common. The Muslim wife indeed has always lived, so far as the law is concerned, under the ever-present shadow of divorce, a shadow mitigated only in comparatively rare cases by certain precautionary devices.[14] It is true, as we have seen, that the unjustified repudiation of an unoffending wife is regarded by the jurists as a sin; but it is none the less held to be legally effective.

There are indeed a number of different ways in which a marriage may be ended in Islamic law, most of which could be loosely classified under the heading of divorce. Some of these are, however, of a somewhat exotic nature seldom known today,[15] and these need not detain us now. It is noteworthy, however, that there are two forms of divorce, both of comparatively (and, in some countries, exceedingly) common occurrence, based on mutual consent. The better known of these, *khul'*, is a dissolution of marriage granted by the husband on the basis of a financial consideration offered by the wife—commonly, but not necessarily, the return of her dower. The second, regarded in some systems as a variety of the first and known as *mubara'a*, represents a dissolution of marriage on the basis of the mutual release of the spouses from any outstanding financial commitments arising from the marriage relationship. In some countries it is exceedingly common for husbands who want to divorce their wives to attempt to provoke them into asking for one of these forms of

[14] See pp. 57–58.
[15] The procedures termed *ila'*, *zihar*, and *li'an*, for instance.

dissolution,[16] in order that they may use the dower (or other sum) so recovered to obtain another wife; but such behavior is explicitly forbidden in the Koran.

Far the most frequent form of divorce in Islamic law is, however, the *talaq,* or unilateral repudiation of a wife by her husband. To the legal validity of this the Sunni jurists, as we have seen, imposed virtually no restriction whatever; so much so that in the Hanafi law formulas of repudiation uttered under the influence of intoxication or intimidation were held legally binding, as were also formulas pronounced as a jest, oath, or threat (although not in sleep or delirium). This meant that not only could a man always divorce his wife if he really wanted to do so, but that many wives found themselves triply divorced by husbands who had no desire whatever to end the marriage relationship. And the Hanafi law was equally extreme in the directly opposite direction: for the Hanafi wife was not only precluded from any unilateral repudiation of her husband, but could not even get a judicial dissolution of her marriage, once consummated, however much her position might be abused. It was in fact the miserable lot of Hanafi wives, as we have seen, which first forced the Ottoman authorities to instigate reforms within the sacrosanct preserves of the family law. It was thus that in 1915 two imperial edicts were issued, the one allowing a Hanafi wife who had been deserted by her husband to demand a judicial dissolution of her marriage, and the other granting her a similar right where her husband proved, unknown to her, to be afflicted with some foul and dangerous disease. After this, progress was rapid, and

[16] E.g., in the Sudan. Cf. *Islamic Law in Africa,* p. 320.

these edicts were followed two years later by the Ottoman Law of Family Rights. This was a fairly comprehensive codification of the law of marriage and divorce which was short-lived in Turkey but which survived much longer in Jordan and Syria, and which is still in force today in Lebanon and Israel.

These reforms greatly improved the lot of married women, in so far as action which they might themselves initiate was concerned; and the Egyptian legislation of 1920 and 1929 went considerably further. As a result, an ill-used wife in Egypt may now claim a judicial divorce on any one of four grounds: that her husband cannot, or will not, support her; that he is afflicted with some disease that makes married life dangerous; that he has left her alone, without legal justification, for at least a year; and that he treats her in a way that makes married life intolerable to one of her social standing.[17] All these reforms—which have in most cases reappeared in the Sudanese Circulars, the Jordanian Law of Family Rights, 1951, the Syrian Law of Personal Status, 1953, and the Moroccan Law of Personal Status, 1958[18]—could find ample justification in the doctrine of one or more of the Sunni schools. These codes also commonly include a provision that, where a wife repeats an allegation of ill-treatment which she cannot substantiate, the court is to appoint the two arbitrators,

[17] Arts. 4–6, 9–11 of Law No. 25 of 1920, Arts. 12, 6–11 of Law No. 25 of 1929, respectively.

[18] Cf. Circular No. 17 (of 1916), Arts. 2–9, 13, and 14–15, together with Circular No. 28 (of 1927), Arts. 2, 4, in the Sudan; Arts. 98–100, 83–90, and 96–97, respectively, in the Jordanian Law; Arts. 110–11, 105–8, 109 and 112–15, respectively, in the Syrian Law; and Arts. 53, 54, 57, and 56, respectively, in the Moroccan Code.

preferably one from each family, prescribed in the Koran for cases of matrimonial discord; and, where reconciliation proves impossible, is to dissolve the marriage on their recommendation either by a simple *talaq* or, where the wife appears primarily to blame, on the basis of some financial consideration which she must provide.[19] It is only the Tunisian Law of Personal Status, 1957, that has gone further than this, and explicitly states that a wife who insists on a divorce for any reason other than one specified in the law will in fact be granted one, but only on the basis of financial compensation decreed by the court.[20]

Some of these reforms have indeed been opposed not only by the conservatives but even by progressive thinkers, on the ground that they weaken the bonds of marriage in circumstances which are not always the husband's fault but may instead be his misfortune. It may, however, be stated in reply that, while a Muslim husband retains his unfettered right of unilateral repudiation, it can do little harm, and may do some good, to open the door of escape more widely than might otherwise be advisable to dissatisfied wives.

The problem of how to restrict a husband's unilateral discretion in this matter has in fact proved much more intractable. It was easy enough to provide, in the Ottoman Law of Family Rights, that formulas of repudiation uttered under the influence of intoxication or intimida-

[19] But the Egyptian reforms, curiously enough, make no provision for such consideration. Cf. Art. 130 of the Ottoman Law, Arts. 6–11 of the Egyptian Law of 1929, Arts. 96–97 of the Jordanian Law, and Arts. 112–15 of the Syrian Law. Art. 25 of the Tunisian Code and Art. 56 of the Moroccan Code are much less precise.

[20] Art. 31(3).

tion would no longer be given any legal effect,[21] since ample authority for this limited reform could be found in the Sunni schools. Much the same could be said regarding formulas pronounced in such a fit of rage as temporarily to deprive the husband of his reason, as provided in the Syrian and Moroccan reforms.[22] It was much bolder to decree that formulas of divorce uttered as an oath or threat should be carried into effect only if the husband really so intended—as in the Egyptian, Sudanese, Jordanian, and Syrian legislation—or should in all cases be disregarded, as in the Moroccan Code;[23] for these reforms cut right across the alleged consensus of Sunni Islam and could only claim a far more tenuous juristic justification. And precisely the same may be said of the provision that the triple divorce, when pronounced in a single formula or on one and the same occasion, should count only as a simple and revocable divorce—a reform introduced in Egypt, the Sudan, Jordan, Syria, and Morocco, and designed to ensure that opportunity for a husband to reconsider a hasty repudiation which was one of the major purposes for the institution of the 'idda period, but of which he had been largely deprived by the "triple" formula and its legal refinements.[24]

It is only in Syria, Morocco, and—still more—Tunisia that the reformers have been bold enough to go further than this. The Syrians were the first to introduce a pro-

[21] Arts. 104–5. These reforms have reappeared in almost all the later codes.

[22] Arts. 89 and 49, respectively.

[23] Art. 2 of Law No. 25 of 1929, Art. 2 of Circular No. 41 of 1936, Art. 70 of the Jordanian Law, and Art. 50 of the Moroccan Code.

[24] Art. 3 of Law No. 25 of 1929, Art. 3 of Circular No. 41 of 1936, Art. 72 of the Jordanian Law, and Art. 51 of the Moroccan Code.

vision that where a wife was divorced without adequate cause and could show that she would suffer damage and poverty as a result, the court might order her husband to pay her a limited sum by way of compensation;[25] and this has been adopted on a wider and more generous scale in Tunisia and Morocco. But the Tunisians have gone further still, and decreed that a divorce will be recognized only if effected in a court of law, which will always order financial compensation where either party unilaterally insists on ending the marriage without such justification as the code allows.[26]

Finally, it should, I think, be mentioned that certain devices were developed by the jurists at a very early date designed to give at least some protection to a Muslim wife in this matter of divorce, whether at her discretion or her husband's. Thus a Muslim wife might always secure the right to end the marriage if she could persuade her husband to delegate to her his right to repudiate her, so that she could divorce herself either in specified circumstances or even at her unfettered discretion.[27] Again, she might persuade him to pronounce a conditional repudiation that would automatically come into operation in certain eventualities. Similarly, some guarantee against frivolous or wanton divorce by the husband might be found in dividing the dower into two parts, the first (and smaller) sum to be paid at the time of the marriage and the other (and larger) sum on widowhood or divorce. It was indeed not uncommon for enlightened fathers to seek to protect

[25] In addition, that is, to the maintenance to which she was always entitled in Hanafi law for the duration of her *'idda* period. Cf. Art. 117.

[26] Art. 31(3).

[27] Although he, too, could still divorce her.

their daughters in one or other of these ways, although they can scarcely have been widely used among the generality of Muslims.

I should perhaps add that I have confined my attention in this lecture to the Middle East, but that somewhat similar facilities for ill-used wives to demand a judicial dissolution of marriage were provided in British India by the Dissolution of Muslim Marriages Act, 1939, although this legislation did nothing to restrict the validity of formulas of repudiation pronounced by Muslim husbands.

. 4 .

THE ISLAMIC LAW
OF INHERITANCE

In explaining my choice of the Islamic law of marriage and divorce as the subject for my previous lecture, I emphasized that this represents at once the very heart of the Shari'a, a salient characteristic of Islamic society down the centuries, a part of the law which is still applied today to the overwhelming majority of the world's four hundred million Muslims, and the center of the present struggle between conservatism and liberalism in Islam.

Now each of these points also applies in its different degree to the Islamic law of inheritance. It too represents the heart of the Shari'a, for it rests more directly than, perhaps, any other aspect of the law on the very text of the Koran, as expanded by certain traditions attributed to the Prophet. Like the law of marriage and divorce, moreover, the Islamic law of inheritance has been characteristic of Islamic society down the ages. Again, this law is still applied throughout almost all the Muslim world, and even —unlike the law of marriage and divorce—to non-Muslim subjects of some Muslim states (e.g., Egypt and Syria).

And in this law too we find a sharp conflict today between the traditionalists and the reformers, although this conflict is rather more technical and legal, and of somewhat less interest to the sociologist, than that concerning questions of marriage and divorce.

It should also be observed that there is no aspect of the law in which the logical and technical excellencies of the Islamic system are more advantageously displayed than in the law of inheritance. Indeed, there is a famous dictum attributed to the Prophet that a knowledge of the shares allotted to the various heirs under this system constitutes the equivalent of one-half of all human knowledge. This saying has often comforted me greatly, seeing that I may at least claim to know more about this half of human knowledge than about the other half! However this may be, it would, I suppose, be true to say that there is no system of inheritance that has been worked out with the detailed thoroughness, the meticulous precision, and the religious devotion—even to the discussion *ad nauseam* of hypothetical problems that could scarcely ever arise in the vicissitudes of real life—which has been accorded so lavishly by Muslim jurists to the Islamic law of succession.

But again, the only satisfactory way to approach this subject is that of setting it in its historical perspective, that is, against the law of pre-Islamic Arabia, in so far as that is known.

Pre-Islamic Arabia, like the bedouin of Arabia today, was organized on a tribal and patriarchal basis. Outside the tribe there was no security other than the unwritten law of the blood feud, under which a man must be avenged, if killed by one of another tribe, by his agnatic relatives, while it was the agnatic relatives of the killer who must, if they wanted to avoid further bloodshed, provide the bloodwite by way of compensation to the "heirs of blood." It was only natural, therefore, that it should be the closest agnates who would also normally succeed to a man's property on death, and that women, cognates, and indeed minors should have no such right. It seems, however, that the practice of making testamentary bequests was fairly widespread, at least in Mecca; and although these bequests had no formal legal validity—for there were no law courts in the formal sense—they would be regarded as the spiritual testament of a dying man, which would normally, no doubt, be respected by his heirs.

In general terms, moreover, the priority between agnates seems to have been such that descendants would exclude both ascendants and collaterals; that ascendants would exclude collaterals; and that, among collaterals, descendants of the father would have priority over descendants of the paternal grandfather, and so on. The only exception to this rule concerns competition between the father's father on the one side and full or consanguine brothers on the other—which has always represented a matter of controversy. Within each "order" (i.e., descendants, ascendants, descendants of father, and descendants of more remote ascendants) the nearer in degree would totally exclude the more remote; and, where claimants were equal both in order and degree, priority would be given to the full blood over the half blood.

Into such a system the advent of Islam introduced certain outstanding reforms. An early verse in the Koran regards it as the obvious duty of a Meccan merchant to make suitable bequests;[1] a slightly later injunction (often termed the "Verse of Bequests") explicitly orders Muslims to make bequests in favor of parents and relatives, that is, in favor, presumably, of mothers, daughters, and others who would have no share under the agnatic system, and in favor of fathers when excluded under that system by sons of the deceased; and a subsequent revelation imposes a similar duty in favor of widows.

It seems, however, that these somewhat vague injunctions did not prove satisfactory, for they were soon followed by detailed instructions as to how much should be given in intestate succession to this relative and that. Thus precise shares were specified in the Koran itself for the widow and widower, for the father and mother, for daughter or daughters, for full and consanguine sisters, and for uterine brothers and sisters—and the Sunni (as distinct from the Shi'i) jurists added the paternal grandfather (on analogy with the father), the "true" grandmother (on analogy with the mother) and the son's daughter (on analogy with the daughter). This does not mean, however, that all these "quota-sharers" are to receive these shares in all cases; on the contrary, when, for instance, the deceased is survived by a son or son's son, none but the surviving spouse, the daughter, and the parents (or, in their absence, the grandparents) will inherit; in the presence of the father, again, no collateral will receive a share; while the consanguine sister will be excluded as a sharer by a brother of the full blood, just as a consanguine brother would have been similarly excluded under the principles applicable to the succession of the *'asaba,* or

[1] Cf. "Wasiya" in *Encyclopedia of Islam,* IV, 1132. The Koranic references are XXXVI, 50; II, 176–77; and II, 241, respectively.

agnates. (These examples of the rules of exclusion are, of course, illustrative rather than exhaustive.) In the case of daughters, of son's daughters, of full and consanguine sisters, and of uterine brothers and sisters, moreover, different shares were specified for a single claimant, on the one hand, and for two or more (to be divided between them), on the other; while in some cases (such as the surviving spouse and the mother) different shares were specified according to whether or not the deceased was survived by a child or even (in the case of the mother only) by "brethren." Nor was the rule that the nearer in degree excludes the more remote applied by the Sunni jurists as rigidly in regard to these quota-sharers as in regard to the agnates: for where the heirs included one daughter and one or more son's daughters, but no corresponding males, they gave the daughter and the son's daughter together the share provided for "daughters" in the plural (i.e. two-thirds), allowed the daughter to take her full single share (i.e. one-half), and gave the son's daughter the difference (i.e. one-sixth). And precisely the same applies to the consanguine sister in the presence of one sister of the full blood but no corresponding males.

But it is essential to observe that the Sunni jurists regarded this institution of quota-sharers as an Islamic reform superimposed on the agnatic system of pre-Islamic Arabia. This meant that entitled sharers would first be given their shares, and then the remainder (as formerly the whole estate) would go to the nearest agnate. But the Sunni jurists also interpreted the relevant Koranic verses as meaning that in four cases only—that of the daughter, son's daughter, and full or consanguine sister—females would now be "agnatized" by corresponding males, tak-

ing half the male share. Thus the daughter coexisting
with a son would take not her quota-share but half the
son's entitlement, and the sister half the entitlement of
an accompanying brother of the same blood. It will be
observed, moreover, that in two cases—that of the father
and father's father—the quota-sharers were themselves
agnates; and here the jurists provided that the father (or,
in default, the father's father) would take only as a sharer
where excluded from the position of nearest agnate by
the presence of a son (or son's son) of the deceased; would
take first as sharer and then, where there was any surplus,
as nearest agnate in the presence of a daughter or son's
daughter; and in all other cases would take as nearest
agnate alone. Finally, the Sunni jurists decided that in two
cases only (that of the full or consanguine sister) females
might take as agnates not only "in the right of" corresponding males, but "in company with" a daughter, or son's
daughter, in the absence of any corresponding males.

But all this must appear exceedingly complicated when
recounted as summarily as this and in abstract terms. Let
me attempt to bring it to life by a few random examples.
Suppose that a man is survived by wife, father, mother,
two sons, one daughter, and an assortment of collaterals.
These last would all be excluded by the presence of the
sons (or indeed of the father); the widow would receive
one-eighth and the father and mother one-sixth each, all
as quota-sharers; and the remainder would be divided between the sons and daughter, with the daughter receiving
half a son's entitlement, as the nearest agnates. Or suppose that a woman is survived by her husband, mother,
daughter, and a distant agnatic cousin. The husband
would receive one-quarter, the mother one-sixth, and the

daughter one-half, all as quota-sharers; and the remainder would go to the cousin, as the nearest agnate. And exactly the same principle would apply if the claimants were limited to a daughter and a remote agnate; for the daughter would take half the estate and the remote agnate the remainder.

In some cases the shares of entitled quota-sharers add up to more than unity; and in such cases the Sunni jurists reduce all these shares pro rata. For example, a woman is succeeded by her husband, father, mother, and two daughters; and in such circumstances the appropriate shares are one-quarter to the husband, one-sixth to both father and mother, and two-thirds to be divided between the two daughters. But these shares add up to an aggregate of fifteen-twelfths (three to the husband, two each to the parents, and eight to the daughters); so they are reduced to unity by the simple expedient of making the total numerator (fifteen) into the new denominator, and thus giving the husband three-fifteenths, the parents two-fifteenths each, and the daughters eight-fifteenths between them. In some few cases, moreover, no agnatic relative whatever is known to exist; and in such cases the Hanafi jurists say that, where there are quota-sharers (other than the surviving spouse), they will take not only their shares but the remainder too, by the doctrine of the "return," in proportion to their respective shares; and that, where there are no quota-sharers either, the whole estate will go to "uterine relatives" (i.e., those relatives who are neither agnates nor quota-sharers) according to an exceedingly complex system. Most modern Shafi'is and all Hanbalis agree, except in regard to the detailed system concerned; but the Malikis make no provision whatever for the return to quota-sharers or for uterine heirs, and in all such cases give the entire estate, or the remainder after entitled quota-sharers have taken their shares, to the public treasury.

Such was the Sunni system in broad outline. But here the Shi'i jurists disagreed radically, and built up a wholly different system out of the same Koranic material, for they took the view that this material should not be regarded as piecemeal reforms superimposed on the old agnatic system but as the basis from which a wholly new system was to be developed. Henceforth the agnates were to have no priority over cognates; instead, each claimant was to have his or her Koranic share—whether specified or (in the case of the son, father, or full or consanguine brother) sometimes by implication—or to take the entitlement of the appropriate quota-sharer or "next of kin" by an elaborate system of representation.

The Shi'is claim, indeed, that their system is more Islamic and more truly Koranic than that of the Sunnis. However that may be, there can be no doubt that the basic reason for this divergence was political rather than juristic. It was the Shi'is' allegiance to the descendants of the Prophet through his daughter Fatima that prompted them to deny any priority of agnates over cognates; and this denial in itself inevitably involved an attempt to expunge the pre-Islamic system and to build up a wholly new system in its place. I use the word "attempt" because, as it seems to me, this did not prove wholly possible; for the silence of the Koran regarding a son when not accompanied by a daughter, a father in cases where there was neither a mother nor a child among the claimants, and a brother without a corresponding sister, makes it difficult not to fall back in some degree on the pre-Islamic system. The final proof, moreover, that the Shi'is were primarily activated by political motives may be found in the special case where a full uncle's son is in competition with a consanguine uncle; for here the Shi'is give the precedence to the full uncle's son, directly contrary to the general rule (which they acknowledge no less than do the Sunnis) that it is only between claimants who are equal in degree that the full blood has preference over the half blood. They themselves, moreover, apply the principle that the nearer in degree will exclude the more remote even in this case if there are other claimants within the same class of heirs; and this solitary exception can be explained only in terms of their allegiance to 'Ali (the Prophet's full uncle's son) in preference to 'Abbas (his consanguine uncle).

In addition, the Shi'is have repudiated a number of other details of the Sunni system that rest on the decisions of the first three caliphs or the deductions of Sunni jurists. They limit the quota-sharers, for instance, to the nine mentioned in the Koran, and deal with the father's father, the grandmother, and the son's daughter, not by regarding them as quota-sharers, but rather as "representing," in suitable circumstances, the son and the parents respectively.

Apart from the surviving spouse (who inherits in all cases), they divide the heirs into three classes:

Class I. (a) Parents. (b) All descendants.

Class II. (a) All ascendants other than parents. (b) All descendants of the parents.

Class III. (a) Paternal uncles and aunts and their descendants—and similarly, great uncles and aunts and their descendants. (b) Maternal uncles and aunts and their descendants—and similarly, great uncles and aunts and their descendants.

Any claimant in Class I will exclude all in Class II, and any claimant in Class II those in Class III. Within Class I and Class II the rule that the nearer in degree will exclude the more remote will operate (where applicable) within sections (a) and (b) respectively, but not between these sections, while in Class III it will operate both within sections (a) and (b) and between them. Within each class the distribution will follow the same basic Koranic principles as those found in the Sunni law, except for a few details of interpretation and application; but the gap filled, in the Sunni system, by the nearest agnate is filled, in that of the Shi'is (in default, that is, of a son, father or brother—or claimant "representing" one of these—in that particular class), by an enormously expanded use of the doctrine of the "return." The Shi'i recourse to the principle of "representation" means, moreover, that they make much more use than do the Sunnis of succession per stirpes rather than per capita; but it is noteworthy that the Shi'is, no less than the Sunnis, reject any doctrine of representation that would conflict with the rule that the nearer in degree excludes the more remote.

The only way to make these seemingly complex rules intelligible is to give them flesh and bones in the form of a few examples. Suppose that a man is succeeded by his mother, daughter, and son's son. In the Sunni system the mother and daughter would receive one-sixth and one-half respectively, as quota-sharers, while the son's son would take the remainder, as nearest agnate. In the Shi'i system, on the other hand, the son's son would be excluded by the daughter, as a descendant nearer in degree; and the mother and daughter would initially take their shares of one-sixth and one-half respectively, and then the remainder proportionally, by the doctrine of the return. Again, suppose a man is succeeded by his son's daughter, his daughter's son, and a distant agnate. In the Sunni system the daughter's son would be excluded as a uterine heir; the son's daughter would take her share of one-half; and the distant agnate would take the remainder. In the Shi'i system, on the other hand, the distant agnate would be excluded, and the son's daughter and daughter's son would represent the son and daughter, and inherit their entitlement of two-thirds and one-third respectively. Or to take one final example: suppose a man is succeeded by his wife, mother, full sister, and consanguine brother. In the Sunni system the wife would take one-quarter, the mother one-sixth and the full sister one-half, all as quota-sharers; and the remaining one-twelfth would go to the consanguine brother, as nearest agnate. In the Shi'i system, on the other hand, the wife would again take her one-quarter, but the mother would take all the rest (first as sharer, and then by the doctrine of the return), since any heir in Class I will exclude all those in Class II.

Let us now turn from these intricacies to something very much simpler. Among both Sunnis and Shi'is there are certain bars to inheritance, such as the fact that the would-be heir is a slave, has caused the death of the *de cujus,* differs from him in religion or (in the case of two non-Muslims) differs from him in domicile. These, I think, demand our passing attention.

We may ignore the bar of slavery, except to observe that there are some parts of the world where it is still relevant. But when we turn to the rule that one who has caused the death of the *de cujus* may not inherit from him, we find that there has been much difference of opinion among the jurists as to the sort of "killing" which will raise this bar. The Hanafis and Shafi'is, for instance, exclude not only the one who has deliberately killed him but also the one who has killed him by accident; and the Hanafis add the further refinement that they have regard only to what may be termed "direct" killing, and do not extend the rule of exclusion to one who encompasses his death by some indirect means. This leads to the strange result that one who leaves poisoned food about even with murderous intent is not debarred from inheriting from his victim, while one who shoots his relative by mere inadvertence is excluded. All the other schools, however, ignore this distinction between direct and indirect killing; and the Malikis, Hanbalis, and Shi'is adopt the rule that only "deliberate" killing (although this may in fact include much that would not be classified as "murder" in this country) will debar the killer from his rights of inheritance.

As for the bar of difference of religion, it must suffice to observe that this rule causes much difficulty and hardship in areas in which members of one family may differ from each other in religious allegiance—for where a Muslim dies (and Islamic law is applied) all non-Muslim relatives will be excluded, while where a non-Muslim dies (and some other law is applied) Muslim relatives will be allowed to inherit. In particular, much hardship is caused in cases of conversion; for where the conversion is from Islam to, say, Christianity, the convert will be excluded, while where the conversion is to Islam, all those relatives who do not follow suit will be debarred. It is only in regard to non-Muslims, however, that the bar of domicile becomes relevant, for it was much debated between the jurists as to whether a non-Muslim domiciled outside the "Abode of Islam"—that is, in the "Abode of War"—might inherit from his coreligionist who was a protected subject of a Muslim state. But this need not detain us here.

One further point. Rights of inheritance are established in Islamic law in all those entitled heirs who are in existence, whether in fact or in law, at the time when the *de cujus* dies—and the phrase "in law" is intended to include a child *en ventre sa mère*. But this clearly raises the problem of deciding at what date a given claimant was in fact conceived. The Sunni jurists solved this problem, in general terms, along common-sense lines: where the mother of the claimant had already been widowed or divorced when the *de cujus* died (or was indeed herself widowed by that death), they applied the maximum period of gestation according to their particular doctrine (two years for the Hanafis, four for the Shafi'is, and five for the Malikis) —on the ground that a child born within this period would be regarded as the legitimate issue of the marriage, so must have been conceived before the marriage ended; but where the mother of the claimant was still married at (and not widowed by) the death of the *de cujus,* they applied the minimum period of gestation (i.e., six months)— on the ground that to adopt any other test would open the door to the possibility that the child had been conceived after the death of the *de cujus,* and that one must not prejudice the entitlement of an established heir in favor of one whose claim is dubious. Some of the Hanbalis alone disagreed with this, and argued that law was concerned with the normal rather than the exceptional, and that the test should therefore be the normal period of gestation (i.e., nine months) rather than the minimum. By the same token, moreover, rights of inheritance and claims to legal paternity go together in other points also; so a child born less than six months after the date of a marriage will not inherit from his father unless the latter specifically acknowledged him as his lawful child.

We must now turn briefly to the law of testate, rather than intestate, succession. Here I shall ignore all details and confine my comments to those broad principles that are essential to an understanding of the Islamic system of inheritance as a whole.

The Islamic law of wills and bequests is founded much less on the Koran than on certain traditions attributed to the Prophet. One of these is accepted by all schools of law as limiting a Muslim's right of testamentary disposition to one-third of his net estate (i.e., of such as is left of his estate after the payment of his debts). This prohibition has been taken in an absolute sense by the Malikis; so, should a testator in fact exceed this limit and his heirs duly execute these bequests, the Maliki jurists regard the excess as a gift from the heirs, rather than a bequest from the deceased. The other schools, however, do not go so far as this, and validate even an excessive bequest provided the heirs agree—an agreement which, according to the Sunni jurists, can validly be given only after the testator's death. This means, of course, that the heirs of a deceased Muslim have a right to their shares (according to the law of intestate succession) in respect of at least two-thirds of his net estate, and this right can be defeated only with their individual consent. Should a testator in fact make a series of bequests that aggregate more than the "bequeathable third" and his heirs withhold their consent, these must be suitably reduced; and this will be done pro rata, according to the Sunni schools, and on a chronological basis, in the Shi'i doctrine.

Another tradition—the terse phrase, "No bequest to an heir"—has had an influence on Islamic law scarcely less profound than that discussed above. This tradition rests in fact on a very dubious foundation even according to Muslim canons of criticism; but it has been accepted as authentic by the alleged "consensus" of Sunni Islam, and interpreted by all the Sunni schools as forbidding a bequest to any who are in fact entitled as heirs on intestacy. Again the Malikis regard this prohibition as absolute, while the other Sunni schools validate even a bequest to an heir provided the other heirs consent after the death of the testator. The Shafi'i jurists allow a testator to make a testament distributing different items of his estate between individual heirs provided this does not mean that any receive more than their due entitlement; but the Hanafis forbid even this. The logic of this prohibition is, of course, that the Sunni jurists regard the shares to which different heirs are entitled as divinely ordained and not subject to any sort of variation at the whim of a testator. Most Sunnis, moreover, regard the "Verse of Bequests" (see p. 62) as having been wholly abrogated by the detailed rules of intestate succession subsequently promulgated and also, as some would say, by this tradition. But the Ithna 'Ashari branch of the Shi'a wholly reject this tradition in its Sunni form, and allow a testator to exercise his unfettered discretion in making bequests—whether to heirs or nonheirs—provided he keeps within the bequeathable third.

When we turn to the law relative to the administration of a deceased Muslim's assets on death, we are immediately struck by the fact that Muslim jurists accord a paramount importance to ensuring, in his own spiritual interests, that all his debts should be duly paid. Thus the Hanafis regard the deceased as fictitiously surviving until the last debt is paid; they deny the heirs any rights whatever over an insolvent estate; and even where they allow the heirs, as a matter of convenience, to distribute or deal with a solvent estate in which certain debts remain outstanding, they insist that creditors who are not in fact paid may, as a last resort, get this distribution annulled and may follow the various items of the estate and recover them even from a bona fide purchaser for value. This principle has been completely reversed in the "Anglo-Mohammedan" Law as applied in India and Pakistan, chiefly as a result of a presumably unintended perversion of Hanafi principles by Mr. Justice Mahmood in Jafri Begam's case.[2] The Shafi'is, instead of postulating the fictitious survival of the deceased, impose a "tacit pledge" on the estate until the debts are paid; but, whatever the device, all schools prefer the claims of the creditors of the deceased to those of a bona fide purchaser for value, that is, they give priority to the spiritual welfare of the deceased over the interests of living claimants, however innocent.

Reforms in the law of testate and intestate succession have been slower to appear than have reforms in the law of marriage and divorce. Even so, the Egyptian parliament promulgated a comprehensive Law of Intestate Succession in 1943 and Law of Testamentary Dispositions in

---

[2] *Jafri Begam* v. *Amir Muhammad Khan* (1885) 7 All. 822.

1946;[3] certain piecemeal reforms along the same lines were adopted at much the same dates in the (then) Anglo-Egyptian Sudan;[4] the Syrian Law of Personal Status, 1953, includes sections concerning both testate and intestate succession;[5] the Tunisian Law of Personal Status, 1957, covers the law of intestate but not testate succession;[6] and the Moroccan Code of Personal Status, 1958, devotes a separate "book" to each subject.[7]

The major achievement in the field of intestate succession has been the mere fact of codification, and the changes effected thereby in the existing law have not been very drastic. The Maliki and Hanbali principle that only "deliberate" homicide—but with no distinction between a "direct" killing and an indirect encompassing of death—will debar the killer from rights of inheritance to the deceased has been accepted, in place of the illogical Hanafi doctrine, wherever this was necessary; and the principle dominant in the Hanafi school, that the father's father should completely exclude full and consanguine brothers, has been similarly discarded. More significant, claims to inheritance based on the maximum period of gestation have been radically reduced by the enactment that no claim will be entertained in respect of a child born more

[3] For details see my articles, "Recent Developments in Shari'a Law" VI and VII, referred to above.

[4] For details see my article, "Recent Developments in Shari'a Law in the Sudan," referred to above, pp. 94–95.

[5] For details see my article, "The Syrian Law of Personal Status," referred to above, pp. 44–48.

[6] For details see my article, "The Tunisian Code of Personal Status," referred to above, pp. 274–75.

[7] My article, "Reforms in Family Law in Morocco," referred to above, does not cover this part of the code.

than a solar year after his mother's widowhood or divorce; while claims to succession by children whose mothers' marriages persisted after the death of the *de cujus* have been favored by the adoption of the Hanbali view that the normal, rather than minimum, period of gestation should be accepted as the criterion in such cases. But the major defect in the Islamic law of succession, namely, the fact that the children of a deceased parent will be completely excluded from any right to inheritance from their grandparent by the survival of an uncle (in Sunni law) or even aunt (in Shi'i law), on the principle that the nearer in degree will exclude the more remote, has proved so formidable that the reformers have been unable as yet to tackle it openly; and an attempt made in Lebanon in 1950 was defeated.

It is in the reforms regarding the law of testamentary dispositions that the major advances have been made. It is in fact by a reform in the law of testate succession that the defect I have just discussed in the Islamic law of intestate succession has found a most ingenious remedy, by the acceptance—first by the Egyptians, then by the Syrians, and later by the Moroccans—of the principle of "Obligatory Bequests." Under this heading the Egyptian Law of Testamentary Dispositions, for example, provides that a grandparent *must* make a bequest to these grandchildren, through any child who has predeceased him, of what this parent would have inherited, on intestacy, had he survived, provided this does not exceed the bequeathable third; that if he fails to do so, the court will act as though he had; and that such "obligatory" bequests will have priority over any "voluntary" bequests that the testator may in fact have made. And the only major difference in the Syrian and Moroccan provisions is that they confine such obligatory bequests to the children of predeceased sons rather than predeceased sons and daughters.

This major reform finds its juristic basis in the claim that the Koranic "Verse of Bequests" was not in fact abrogated by the "Verses of Inheritance," at least in so far as close relatives who are excluded from any right of inheritance are concerned; in the view of certain early jurists that to make such bequests is still a duty, and that in default a judge should, if necessary, take from other legatees to provide them; and that the ruler has the right to specify which of such possible claimants should be preferred.

The other major change in the law of testate succession is confined to the Egyptian and Sudanese reforms, namely, that a Muslim may now make bequests within the bequeathable third to whom he will, whether heirs or nonheirs, regardless of whether his heirs (or other heirs) may, or may not, consent. This runs directly counter to the alleged consensus of Sunni Islam, and looks suspiciously like an adoption of Ithna 'Ashari views. But the reformers urge in its support that the tradition "No bequest to an heir" is poorly attested; is sometimes followed by the words "except within the bequeathable third"; and might in any case be construed as abrogating the command— rather than the right— to make such bequests. In addition, they point to the circumstances and requirements of modern life.

In conclusion I shall briefly review some of the defects— real or alleged—in the Islamic law of succession that must be balanced against its undoubted excellencies. These may perhaps be summarized as follows:

First, the widow receives very inadequate treatment, for her maximum share is one-quarter of her husband's estate, and this is in most cases reduced to one-eighth by the survival of any child of the deceased. Should there be co-wives, moreover, this share is divided between them. Since, however, this rests on the explicit text of the Koran, the reformers have felt unable to do anything about it, except for the Egyptian provision allowing bequests even to an heir. The situation can, however, be somewhat remedied by the device of providing for a large sum as deferred dower, payable on widowhood or divorce.

Second, the rule against representation of a deceased heir—at least where the children of such heir would be excluded on the principle that the nearer in degree excludes the more remote—causes much hardship. This is a serious defect, but one which again the reformers have felt unable to face openly (for Mohammed himself, it seems, suffered from its application). But we have already seen how it has been substantially remedied, in so far as grandchildren are concerned, by the indirect device of obligatory bequests.

Third, the Islamic system is excessively rigid, for the shares of the possible heirs are all exactly prescribed, regardless of the fact that their deserts may vary enormously in real life according to individual circumstances, for example, that some are virtuous and some profligate, or that some are destitute and others opulent. Only in Egypt and the Sudan (and among the Ithna 'Asharis) has this been mitigated by the possibility of making bequests within the bequeathable third even to an heir. (In the past, of course, the *waqf* system was widely used, and frequently abused, in order to give the founder the opportunity to distribute the income among his heirs at his discretion; but this is no longer possible in Egypt or Syria, and the right has been severely limited in Lebanon.)

Fourth, the emphasis in Sunni law on the agnates is today an anachronism. This system was no doubt reasonable enough in the tribal life of early Islam; but it is largely irrelevant to modern life, where a man whose heirs are an only daughter and a distant agnate (whom he may not know, or may heartily dislike) will resent the fact that the latter will inherit half his estate. But again the reformers have not yet taken any action in this matter, except for the Egyptian innovation regarding bequests to heirs; and here the Shiʻi system seems much more suited to modern life.

Fifth, the Islamic law of inheritance leads to excessive fragmentation of real estate, which soon becomes subdivided into plots of an uneconomical size. This has been avoided in some countries by legislation requiring the registration of all claims to real estate, and by regulations forbidding the registration of plots of less than a specified size; with the effect that heirs are forced to come to some amicable arrangement whereby the real estate passes to some heirs only, and the others take their share (or compensation) from other property, or else the estate is sold and the price distributed among the heirs as a whole. It is noteworthy, however, that many Muslim writers stress the virtues of the Islamic law of inheritance as a guarantee against the perpetuation of large estates, whether in land or other forms of wealth; and even, when coupled with the law of *zakat,* or compulsory alms, as providing a *via media* between capitalism and socialism. But this claim need not be taken too seriously.

Sixth, the rule that there is no inheritance between those who differ in religion often causes injustice and inconvenience. This rule is applied by the Shi'is only to the advantage of the Muslim community and the disadvantage of non-Muslims, whereas the Sunnis apply it both ways without discrimination. All the same, the rule often causes distress and injustice—particularly, as has been noted, in parts of the world where members of one family are apt to be divided in their religious allegiance. Many attempts have been made to tackle this problem by statute law in countries such as Tanganyika and Nyasaland,[8] while the claims of converts have been boldly (although inconsistently) upheld by such legislation as the Indian Caste Disabilities Removal Act, 1850. The Middle East reformers have hitherto left the problem severely alone, mitigated only by the corresponding rule that there is no objection in Islamic law to a Muslim making testamentary dispositions in favor of one who follows a different religion.

[8] Cf. Administration (Small Estates) (Amendment) Ordinance and Marriage, Divorce, and Succession (non-Christian Asiatics) (Amendment) Ordinance, both of 1947, in Tanganyika; and Asiatics (Marriage, Divorce, and Succession) Ordinance, 1929, in Nyasaland. For details see *Islamic Law in Africa,* pp. 124–27, 162–63.

. 5 .

CONTEMPORARY LEGAL
TRENDS IN THE MUSLIM
WORLD

The first lecture emphasized the basic differences between Islamic law and law as we know it in the West.
We saw that Western law, which largely represents an
amalgam of legislation and case law, is essentially a human law, which responds, whether more or less quickly
and effectively, to the ever-changing patterns of social and
economic life; whereas Islamic law constitutes, in theory
at least, a divine law, which is essentially immutable and
which provides a norm to which Muslim society is always
required to conform.

In the second lecture we considered the situation as we
find it in the Middle East today. We saw that the law in
these countries is in fact by no means static, but rather
that enormous changes in their legal and judicial systems
have been effected over the last century. In part this has
been achieved by putting Islamic law substantially on one
side, in all but the law of personal status and family relations, in most of these countries, and in part by effecting

reforms in Islamic law itself, as still applied by the courts in the sacred sphere of family law, by means of a series of ingenious expedients.

Next we turned, for two lectures, to consider two particular aspects of Islamic law—the law of marriage and divorce and the law of inheritance—in rather greater detail. And we chose these particular topics partly because it is the family law that has always represented the very heart of the Shari'a, partly because this law has been characteristic of the structure and ethos of Islamic civilization down the centuries, partly because this is a sphere in which Islamic law is still actually applied by the courts throughout almost the entire Muslim world, and partly because it is precisely at this point that the battle is now joined between the forces of conservatism and of progress.

Now we come to the last of these lectures, "Contemporary Legal Trends in the Muslim World"; and it is my purpose to take another look at some of the changes we have already reviewed, to extend our consideration to a few other parts of the Muslim world, and to see if we cannot discern the emergence of some sort of pattern, and even hazard a forecast as to the direction or directions in which future developments are likely to go.

Hitherto in these lectures we have in the main concentrated our attention on such countries as Egypt and the Sudan, Lebanon and Syria, Jordan and Iraq, Tunisia and Morocco. In large part it is these countries that will concern us again now; but let us at least start by taking a rather more comprehensive view of the Muslim world, in order that we may attempt to discern the various legal trends that prevail today in its different parts.

The legal systems of the Muslim world may be broadly

divided today into three groups: (1) those that still regard the Shari'a as the fundamental law and still apply it more or less in its entirety; (2) those that have abandoned the Shari'a and have substituted a wholly secular law; and (3) those that have reached some compromise between these two positions.

Of those countries which have hitherto retained the Shari'a as their fundamental law and still attempt to apply it throughout the whole range of human relationships, Saudi Arabia and the Northern Region of Nigeria will serve as examples—although Yemen, Oman, or Afghanistan might also be cited.

Saudi Arabia is typical of an independent Muslim country that still pays at least lip service to the Shari'a as governing every aspect of life. It has not "received" any system of foreign law; and it has promulgated very little legislation of Western inspiration. Indeed, any legislation contrary to the fundamental concepts of Islam would in theory be equally contrary to the Fundamental Law of the Hijaz promulgated by the late King 'Abd al-'Aziz Ibn Saud, for Article 6 reads: "Legislation in the Kingdom of the Hijaz shall always conform to the Book of God, the Sunna of his Prophet and the conduct of the Prophet's Companions and pious Followers." But although the Kingdom of Saudi Arabia is officially committed to the Wahhabi variety of Hanbali doctrine, it has been authoritatively stated that there is no objection to the principles of some other school of Sunni Islam being preferred in suitable circumstances, by command of the king.[1]

[1] *Government's First Memorial* in the Arbitration Between the Government of Saudi Arabia and the Arabian American Oil Company, App. I, 10–11.

Yet even in Saudi Arabia this does not today represent the whole story. Even under the late king a commercial *nizam*, or ordinance, was promulgated and a Council of Merchants set up in Jidda to settle disputes regarding commercial transactions according to the principles of the Ottoman Commercial Code of 1850. More recently an income tax decree, in the drafting of which an American expert in the field of taxation took a prominent part, was enacted; and this represents an amalgam of the Islamic principles regarding the *zakat*, or obligatory alms, with American notions of fiscal legislation. It is significant, moreover, that royal decrees are today assuming an ever-increasing importance in the life of the country. There can indeed be no manner of doubt that this process will tend to gather speed, for Saudi Arabia is likely to become more and more closely drawn into the orbit of international—and particularly American—commercial interests.

When we turn to the Northern Region of Nigeria we are confronted by a situation that is again typical, from one point of view, of those parts of the Muslim world where the Shari'a is still regarded as the fundamental law and is applied in almost every sphere of life, yet is also, from another angle, almost wholly without parallel. For Northern Nigeria is unique among these "conservative" Muslim countries in having a very large non-Muslim minority and in the fact that the Islamic criminal law, as still applied (with certain restrictions) in the courts of the Muslim emirates, coexists with a criminal law (the Nigerian Criminal Code) of an entirely different origin and inspiration, enacted and administered by the British. This leads to the strange result that even in homicide cases two widely divergent systems of law are both applied—the one by one set of courts, and the other by another; that it is often almost a matter of chance under which system an accused person will be tried; and that this in turn will often lead to diametrically different decisions in regard both to conviction and sentence. This is unsatisfactory, to say the least.[2]

But exactly the same may be said of the Islamic law of homicide itself, as enunciated in the texts of the Maliki school which are locally accepted as authoritative—at least in terms of a population of mixed faiths; for not only is the definition of deliberate homicide (for which the death penalty is applicable on the demand of the heirs of blood) very much wider than the sort of homicide for which the death penalty is prescribed under the code, but provocation—even of the most extreme variety—is wholly irrelevant, and the blood of a Muslim is regarded as of so much greater value than that of a non-Muslim that the heirs of blood of a Christian or pagan may never demand that a Muslim murderer should be executed. This throws into bold relief the unsuitability of Islamic law (except perhaps in its Hanafi variety) as a law of homicide for a mixed community.

The same is also true of the Islamic law of crime as a whole—for this largely contents itself with an exact definition of a few major offenses (for which alone penalties are precisely prescribed, sometimes of a nature which would be considered inhuman today, which can in practice very seldom properly be imposed, on account of the almost im-

---

[2] For details see *Islamic Law in Africa*, pp. 171–224; my article "Law and Custom in Muslim Areas in Africa: Recent Developments in Nigeria," *Civilisations*, VII (1957), and my article, "Conflict of Laws in Northern Nigeria," *Journal of African Law*, I (1957), 87–98.

possible standard of proof required), while the punishment of all other wrongdoing is left to the discretion of the executive or judiciary. This not only leads to the widest divergencies between court and court, but also gives rise to allegations of injustice and oppression (whether true or false) on the part of political offenders.

And the Islamic system of procedure is equally unsuited to a progressive community of varied religious allegiance. Framed to be largely self-operating, it is based on rigid rules as to the admissibility or inadmissibility of evidence (rather than common-sense principles as to the credibility of such evidence), under which the evidence of non-Muslims is very seldom admissible in any case involving Muslim litigants, the evidence of women is never accepted in regard to any criminal charge, and the evidence of an interested party is wholly rejected.

It will then cause little surprise that a Panel of Jurists, appointed by the Northern Nigerian government in August, 1958, and on which I had the honor to serve, advised that Islamic law as such should be confined in Northern Nigeria (as in the vastly greater part of the Muslim world, and especially in mixed communities) to questions of personal status and the family relations of Muslim litigants; that the Islamic law of contract and tort should be applied, where suitable, only as the law under which the parties in fact concluded their contract or as the law of civil wrongs locally accepted by custom; and that the Maliki law of crime and procedure should be abandoned in favor of a criminal code which had proved acceptable to millions of Muslims in other countries and principles of procedure designed to ensure substantial justice. It is understood, moreover, that the Northern Nigerian government has decided to accept these recommendations. If this proves to be the case, it means that yet another Muslim region, hitherto of a markedly conservative and traditional character, is now to come into line with those developments which, as we have seen, have been taking place in most of the Arab countries throughout the last century.

But before we turn once more to these Arab countries which have been our major concern throughout these lectures, we must notice in passing that part of the Muslim world which has, officially at least, turned entirely secular. It is precisely at this point that Turkey presents a complete contrast to countries such as Saudi Arabia. In the latter, as we have seen, the Shari'a is still accepted as the fundamental law in public as in private life, while in the former it has been officially abandoned, in so far as the courts are concerned, even in the sphere of family relations. At the inception of the revolution, it is true, the Ataturk regime envisaged the promulgation of new codes of law derived from Turkey's Islamic heritage, but when month after month passed in futile disputes between the members of the committee set up for this purpose, the government lost patience. It was at this juncture that their determination to align their country with the European rather than the Eastern world, their insistence on liberation from the shackles of the past and a bold advance along the path of social progress, and their conviction that the situation was too urgent to permit the drafting of new, indigenous codifications led the government to the drastic expedient of adopting European codes almost verbatim.[3]

[3] Cf. H. Timur, "The Place of Islamic Law in Turkish Law Reform," *Annales de la Faculté de Droit d'Istanbul*, VI (1956), 76; also *Die Welt des Islams*, N.S., II (1953), 211.

It was thus that in 1926 the Swiss Code was substituted for the Shari'a, even in the sphere of family law; that monogamy replaced polygamy; and that judicial divorce—on certain specified grounds, which were the same for either party—was substituted for the husband's unilateral repudiation or the mutual consent of the spouses.

None the less, the vast majority of the Turks remain convinced Muslims. Even among the ruling classes the majority would maintain that they had not abandoned Islam, but that they had adopted the Western attitude that religion should be a personal matter between the individual and his God rather than a system of law imposed by the state; and there can be no doubt that the common people have little understanding of such distinctions. Not only so, but in the villages of Anatolia marriages and divorces on the Islamic pattern continue alongside (and greatly outnumber) marriages under the code. This is partly because people sometimes want to marry at an earlier age than the law allows (although the minimum ages for marriage as originally promulgated have themselves been reduced by subsequent legislation); [4] partly because they still desire on occasions to contract polygamous unions; partly because they prefer a form of marriage that can be ended by unilateral repudiation; partly because they do not want to incur the trouble and expense of traveling considerable distances to obtain the necessary health certificates and fulfill the other statutory requirements of

[4] Law No. 3453 of 1938. Cf. H. V. Velidedeoglu, "Problèmes de la Réception du C. C. S. en Turquie," in *Annales* (1956), 114; also G. Jäschke, "Die Imam-Ehe in der Türkei," *Die Welt des Islams*, N.S., IV, 189. Cf. also H. V. Velidedeoglu, "The Reception of Foreign Law in Turkey," *International Social Science Bulletin*, IX (1957), p. 63.

a civil marriage; and partly because it is the marriage before a Muslim imam, however unrecognized by the law, that retains a greater social prestige in the villages than the statutory form of marriage. On a number of occasions, moreover, the legislature has been forced to recognize the position by promulgating legislation legitimizing the issue of these "informal" unions, and even regularizing the unions themselves provided they were in fact monogamous.[5]

All the same, it seems that the code is today making progress, even if slow, at the expense of traditional behavior. This is, of course, quite contrary to the theory of many sociologists, who insist—with some reason—that legislation which is entirely contrary to social habits, and is not supported by any significant body of public opinion, will remain ineffective. Curiously enough, it seems that the Korean War has proved a major influence in favor of the code, for it was soon discovered that it was only a legal marriage which would justify marriage allowances and widows' pensions. And the fact that the soldiers came from a broad cross section of the community meant that their influence was widespread.[6]

But to return to those Arab countries—such as Egypt and the Sudan, Lebanon and Syria, Jordan and Iraq, Tunisia and Morocco—which have taken the middle path between the two extremes of retaining Islamic law, nominally at least, in its entirety and abandoning it, officially

---

[5] E.g., Law No. 2330 of 1933, Law No. 4727 of 1945, Law No. 5524 of 1950, and Law No. 6652 of 1956. Cf. G. Jäschke, *Die Welt des Islams,* N.S., IV, 184 ff.; also *ibid.,* V (1957), 115.

[6] Cf. H. Timur, "Civil Marriages in Turkey: Difficulties, Causes, and Remedies," *International Social Science Bulletin,* IX (1957), p. 36.

at least, completely. In the second lecture I reviewed the major reforms that have been effected in the law as it is applied in these countries, but I have left until this last lecture the attempt to trace the pattern these reforms seem to be taking and to make a diagnosis of contemporary trends. Let me remind you then of the major features in this process of reform.

The first stage, you may remember, was the introduction—from about 1850—of a clear-cut dichotomy in the law, part of which was covered by codes of predominantly Western inspiration, while part remained under the unchallenged sway of the Shari'a. It is true that a tacit dichotomy of this sort had in fact existed down the centuries throughout the Muslim world; but never before had it been so frank and recognized. Under this dichotomy the criminal and commercial law became almost wholly secularized, while the family law remained rigidly Islamic. But it is only just to observe that this dichotomy was never complete in regard to the substantive law, for the Majalla was retained for many years as the civil code of the Ottoman Empire, and the Majalla was a codification, on more or less Western principles, of Islamic precepts; and even in Egypt (where the Majalla was never applied) the civil codes, while predominantly French in origin, included a number of provisions taken from the Shari'a.

It was indeed in the sphere of the courts and their personnel that the dichotomy was most striking of all. For while the Shari'a courts continued to be staffed by ulema of the old type, trained in the traditional schools how to extract from the ancient texts that dominant opinion of the Hanafi school which the state had commanded them to follow, the secular courts were presided over by judges educated in the Western manner and often even in the countries of the West. The influence of the mixed courts, moreover, tended steadily to emphasize this development and deepen the influence of Western legal thought on the growing body of civil lawyers.

The next stage was not reached until more than half a century later. But from 1915 onward, you may remember, the process of reform was extended even to the family law of Islam. But in this sphere—by contrast with the more general law—there was no open secularization; instead, the law of the family remained officially Islamic, and those reforms regarded as essential were introduced by means of three major expedients. The first of these was the device of refusing any judicial recognition, or enforcement, to certain claims which the Shari'a would have upheld; the second was the principle that, instead of enforcing the dominant Hanafi doctrine in every particular, the legislature (or executive) might specify certain variant doctrines, as advocated by some other school or jurist, which were to be applied in its place; and the third was the promulgation of administrative regulations to supplement the Shari'a, and their enforcement by means of penal sanctions.

It was the second of these expedients that was not only most commonly used but also destined to have the most far-reaching influence. For its extensive adoption inevitably led to the progressive codification of the relevant law—with the dual result that the Shari'a law, as applied by the courts, took on an increasingly modern appearance and also became such as could be administered, not only by jurists trained in the lore of the ancient texts, but also by the graduates of modern law schools.

This development, moreover, seems to me to have be-
tokened, or at least to have run parallel to, a radical
change of thinking in the countries concerned. In the
second lecture I remarked that whereas to the Western
mind the progressive displacement of the Shari'a by Western codes might appear to be the most drastic expedient
possible, to the conservative Muslim of the end of the last
century this was not in fact the case. On the contrary, it
seemed to him preferable to maintain the Shari'a in its
purity and entirety as the ideal law for the golden age,
even if this meant abandoning it in practice for a secular
law forced upon him by the exigencies of modern life,
rather than to permit any profane meddling with its immutable provisions. This attitude was in fact only a particular application of the general rule that to a Muslim
it is far less heinous to ignore or disobey the divine law
than to run any risk of questioning or denying it.

But this attitude could scarcely survive the necessity to
reform even that part of the law which was still specifically Islamic, and which, it was felt, must remain so.
This is, I think, obvious on general principles; but it is
significant also that these later reforms were introduced
with at least the tacit, and usually the active, co-operation
of the ulema. It is true, of course, that many of them regarded these reforms with ill-concealed repugnance; but
their acquiescence was secured not only by pressure from
above but also by their growing conviction that the only
alternative to the reform of the Shari'a was its complete
abandonment.

And this change of attitude led naturally to the parallel
development which we have noted in regard to the civil
law; namely, the growing sentiment that, instead of bor-

rowing a foreign code, a system of law adequate for modern life might be derived from the principles of the Shari'a alone, if only these were manipulated with sufficient flexibility; or, alternatively, that principles so derived could be incorporated in a code, much more extensively than in the past, alongside others that were of alien origin and inspiration. It is indeed this last (and more moderate) attitude that represents the philosophy behind the new civil codes in Egypt, Syria, and Iraq.

But these two parallel developments during recent years themselves betoken, it seems to me, a softening of the dichotomy in the law which was so manifest and clear-cut from about 1850 till 1915. For today both the civil and the Shari'a law are largely codified and promulgated in the form of legislative enactments. Even the Shari'a law, moreover, is now being infiltrated by concepts derived largely from the West, for example, the prohibition of child-marriage, the limitation or prohibition of polygamy, and the restriction of a husband's right of unfettered, unilateral repudiation—although the resultant reforms may assume an Islamic dress and claim an Islamic pedigree. Similarly, as we have seen, the civil law is becoming somewhat more permeated by principles derived wholly or in part from the Shari'a. So the stage seems to be set for a substantial narrowing of the gulf between the two systems of law and between the courts that administer them.

It is deeply significant, moreover, that this development runs parallel with a powerful upsurge of nationalism in most of the countries concerned. Nor is this nationalism exclusively directed toward the outside; instead, it also looks inward and covets an internal consolidation of the state and its administration. It was only natural, therefore, that the revolutionary regime now in power in Egypt should have effected what had often been discussed and desired in the past, but as often postponed because of the opposition it provoked, namely, the suppression of the community courts of the various Christian and Jewish communities and the centralization of justice in the hands of the national courts.[7] Many of these community courts had indeed been far from satisfactory in regard both to their efficiency and integrity, while disputes about jurisdiction had been endemic. But the government also took the bold step of abolishing the Shari'a courts at the same time,[8] partly, no doubt, to repudiate any charge of religious discrimination, and partly on the ground of two recent scandals in these courts (which were given the widest publicity, apparently in order to prepare public opinion for this drastic innovation).

But in spite of the fact that the specifically religious courts have been abolished in Egypt, the personal law of each community is still applied in such matters as marriage and divorce by the national courts—with the help, where necessary, of expert advice. As for the Qadis of the Shari'a courts, they were in most cases re-employed in the national courts, where they still continue to handle cases involving the personal status or family law of Muslim litigants. At first sight it would seem, therefore, that little fundamental change has been effected in so far as the Shari'a is concerned. I believe, however, that this impres-

[7] For another development of this argument—indeed a prophecy of this unification of the courts before the die was cast in Egypt—see my article, "Law Reform in the Muslim World," *International Affairs,* XXXII (1956), 51.

[8] See G. N. Sfeir, "The Abolition of Confessional Jurisdiction in Egypt," *The Middle East Journal,* X (1956), 248–56.

sion would be erroneous; for it is most unlikely that judges with the training and background of the previous Shari'a Qadis will in future be appointed to the national courts, so it would appear to be only a question of time before cases of personal status are tried exclusively by judges with a modern and secular training. Somewhat similar changes have, moreover, recently been effected in Tunisia.[9] It is interesting in this context to recall that as long ago as 1917 the Ottoman Law of Family Rights had included special sections for Jews and Christians, and had had as one of its main objectives the concentration of all litigation in the hands of the national courts; but these sections were omitted when this law was brought into operation in Syria, Lebanon, Jordan, and Palestine (as it then was) because of the opposition of the non-Muslim communities, and this law as there enacted applied only to Muslims.

It seems clear, moreover, that—apart from a successful revivalist movement in Islam (which could scarcely in any case have more than local and temporary significance in terms of the modern world)—this tendency to centralize all litigation in the hands of unified national courts will spread in time to other Arab countries. Such courts, moreover, will require the complete codification of the personal law and will approach its application from an increasingly secular standpoint. It seems probable indeed that the civil codes of the future will cover marriage, divorce, guardianship, and succession alongside the law of contract, tort, partnership, and so forth, with the proviso

[9] The unification of the courts was indeed one of the main objectives of the Tunisian reforms. See my article, "The Tunisian Code of Personal Status" referred to above, pp. 262 ff.

that whereas, in the latter, principles derived from European law will tend to predominate, although intermingled with provisions taken from the Shari'a, in the former Islamic principles will prevail, although permeated in some respects by ideas of an alien inspiration.

There can be little doubt that the secularization of the law (in large part at least) is here to stay, since lawyers, judges, and legislators are all increasingly drawn from the ranks of those who have received a Western and secular education. The classical Muslim attitude that the divine law is supreme, and binds the Sultan as much as the subject, was all too commonly ignored in practice in past centuries but was seldom, if ever, challenged in principle. But to a modern national democracy the sovereignty of the people and the unfettered authority of legislation enacted in accordance with constitutional requirements stand on a different dogmatic level; and the military dictatorships that are fast taking the place of democracies in these countries seem always to proclaim that same sovereignty of the people, however much they limit and safeguard the ways in which that sovereignty is to be expressed.

All the same, problems abound. How far is the law of the different Arab states to be unified—and, if so, on what basis? How far is this law to be derived from Islamic principles, and on what foundation? Will the Muslim world be content with the present expedients? To effect reforms by means of the procedural device of making no attack whatever on the substantive law, but refusing to allow its enforcement—in specified circumstances—by the national courts, has provided an admirable method in the past; but may it not have outlived its usefulness? To select those opinions, or half-opinions, of the great jurists of the past which are best adapted to modern life and put them together in a code, entirely regardless of the fact that many of these heterogeneous opinions rest on completely contradictory juristic premises and arguments, has proved deeply beneficial in practice, but seems unsatisfactory in theory. It would be better, one would think, to give frank and unqualified recognition to the validity of contemporary *ijtihad*, or the reinterpretation of the ancient texts by modern scholars. This would, of course, involve an equally frank repudiation of the binding force of consensus as this has been claimed down the centuries—or, indeed, of the very existence of any true consensus, except perhaps on a few basic points; but for this rejection the foundation has already been laid by many writers. And it is probable that mere reinterpretation of itself would not suffice, but would have to be augmented by the doctrine that certain precepts must be regarded as of only temporary or passing significance; or that changes in circumstances may have justified, or even necessitated, a change in the law.

Such considerations are indeed particularly relevant to the law of international relations and such matters as fundamental rights. Here the classical doctrines of Islamic law are wholly and manifestly irreconcilable with modern international law, with membership of the United Nations, and with the Declaration of Human Rights. The normal attitude of the modern Muslim is to ignore this incompatibility, or to take refuge in assertions—valid enough in themselves—that the Muslims had an international law, very enlightened in some respects, long before that of the Western world, that the Muslim empires often accorded better treatment to religious minorities than did their Christian contemporaries, and that the Koran itself prescribes that there should be "no compulsion in religion." It is time, however, that they should frankly face the fact that to all the classical jurists the non-Muslim was by no means the equal of the Muslim either in legal or in political privileges; that religious liberty meant freedom for one born in another religion to continue to practice that religion in an unobtrusive manner or to abandon it in favor of Islam, not for the Muslim to adopt any other faith; and that the Koranic verses denouncing force in matters of religion were abrogated by others commanding the *jihad,* or religious war, until the whole world had been brought under the political dominance of Islam. There have as yet been very few Muslims bold enough to assert, for example, that these later revelations must be regarded as of only temporary and relative significance, while the earlier and more tolerant verses must be taken as the basic and enduring rule.

There can be no doubt, moreover, that many Muslim countries of the modern type would like to get rid of a different law of marriage and divorce for Muslims, Christians, and Jews and introduce a unified law for all nationals regardless of their religion. The new Tunisian Code of Personal Status, indeed, is so enlightened that the Tunisian Jewish community has been willing to accept it, and it is now the general law for all Tunisians. It must be remembered, however, that there are very few Tunisian Christians; and that the Christian communities in most Arab countries would strenuously oppose a law that permits divorce, provided it is effected before a court of law, either by mutual consent or on the insistence of either party. It seems clear that to achieve a common law of marriage and divorce in such countries would necessarily involve a violation of either Muslim or Christian sentiments.

There is, of course, a considerable body of "secularists" on both sides who would be prepared to sit down and agree upon those principles with regard to marriage and divorce which appeared to them most conducive to the public welfare, and to leave it to the different religious authorities to persuade their adherents to conform to such stricter rules as their religion might require (or to claim, in the name of religious theory, a freedom the state would not in practice permit). This may in fact come about in the course of time; but it will involve a further severance between church and state in a way that is fundamentally alien to Muslim ideology. And while the great majority of the people remain convinced, if ignorant, Muslims, who believe that Mohammed was sent with the divine mission of introducing a final and authoritative law which is incumbent on all believers, too wide and open a discrepancy between the law of Islam and the law of the state will inevitably accentuate that divided loyalty which already exists. This must be faced.

It is precisely at this point that the Pakistan experiment assumes such interest for the whole Muslim world. True, the Pakistanis will no doubt be content to allow non-Muslims to follow their own personal law in matters of family relations for many years to come, while any radical reform of the Islamic personal law appears to have been temporarily shelved. But the constitution—now, of course, abrogated—explicitly provided that legislation (both current and future) must be brought into conformity with the "Koran and Sunna," and a Law Reform Commission had been duly constituted to consider how this provision could best be brought into effect.

The commission was faced indeed with basic problems of the most fundamental nature. What verses in the Koran are relevant; how many have been abrogated; and how are those verses which are still authoritative to be interpreted? How is the Sunna of the Prophet to be established; which traditions are authentic; and how are they to be interpreted? The traditional answer of all the schools to these questions is, of course, the consensus of the jurists; but the Pakistani constitution makes no mention of this, and the traditional view would involve such a return to the Middle Ages as progressive Pakistanis would never tolerate. It seems, however, that the present military rule will have brought the work of the commission (and perhaps the very need for its activities) to an abrupt end. And while this is without doubt disappointing to the theorist, it is difficult to avoid the conclusion that it may in fact prove to have been in the popular interests—at this juncture—of both Pakistan and the whole Muslim world.

SELECT BIBLIOGRAPHY
of Books and Articles
on Islamic Law in English and French

Abdur Rahim. *Muhammadan Jurisprudence*. Madras, 1911.

Abdur Rahman, A. F. M. *Institutes of Mussalman Law*. Calcutta, 1907.

Aghnides, N. P. *Mohammedan Theories of Finance* (especially "Introduction to Mohammedan Law"). New York, 1916.

Amedroz, H. F. "The Office of Kadi in the Ahkam Sultaniyya of Mawardi." *Journal of the Royal Asiatic Society*, 1910.

———. "The Mazalim Jurisdiction in the Ahkam Sultaniyya of Mawardi." Ibid., 1911.

———. "The Hisba Jurisdiction in the Ahkam Sultaniyya of Mawardi." Ibid., 1916.

Ameer Ali. *Mahommedan Law*, I (4th edition). Calcutta, 1912.

———. Ibid., II (5th edition). Calcutta, 1929.

Anderson, J. N. D. *Islamic Law in Africa*. London, 1954.

———. "Recent Developments in Shari'a Law in the Sudan." *Sudan Notes and Records*, XXI, 1, 1950.

———. "Irregular and Void Marriages in Hanafi Law." *Bulletin of the School of Oriental and African Studies*, XIII, 2, 1950.

———. "Recent Developments in Shari'a Law" I–X. Successive numbers of the *Muslim World*, XL, 4, 1950–XLII, 4, 1952.

Anderson, J. N. D. "Homicide in Islamic Law." *Bulletin of the School of Oriental and African Studies,* XIII, 4, 1951.

——. "The Religious Element in Waqf Endowments." *Journal of the Royal Central Asian Society,* 1951.

——. "The Personal Law of the Druze Community." *Die Welt des Islams,* N.S. II, 1–2, 1952.

——. "A Draft Code of Personal Law for 'Iraq." *Bulletin of the School of Oriental and African Studies,* XV, 1, 1953.

——. "The Shari'a and Civil Law (the Debt Owed by the New Civil Codes of Egypt and Syria to the Shari'a)." *Islamic Quarterly,* I, 1, 1954.

——. *The Relevance of Oriental and African Legal Studies* (Inaugural lecture). Published by the School of Oriental and African Studies. London, 1954.

——. "The Syrian Law of Personal Status." *The International and Comparative Law Quarterly,* VII, 1955.

——. "Tropical Africa: Infiltration and Expanding Horizons." *Unity and Variety in Muslim Civilization* (ed. G. E. Von Grunebaum). Chicago, 1955.

——. "Customary Law and Islamic Law in British African Territories." *The Future of Customary Law in Africa.* Leiden, 1956.

——. "Law Reform in the Middle East." *International Affairs,* XXXII, 1, 1956.

——. "Reflections on Law: Natural, Divine and Positive." *Journal of Transactions of the Victoria Institute,* LXXXVIII, 1956.

——. "Law as a Social Force in Islamic Culture and History." *Bulletin of the School of Oriental and African Studies,* XX, 1957.

——. "Conflict of Laws in Northern Nigeria." *Journal of African Law,* I, 2, 1957.

——. "Law and Custom in Muslim Areas in Africa: Recent Developments in Nigeria." *Civilisations* (Brussels), VII, 1, 1957.

——. "The Tunisian Law of Personal Status." *The International and Comparative Law Quarterly,* VII, 1958.

——. "Reforms in Family Law in Morocco." *Journal of African Law,* II, 3, 1958.

——. "The Family Law of Turkish Cypriots." *Die Welt des Islams,* N.S.V., 3–4, 1958.

Anderson, J. N. D., and Coulson, N. J. "The Moslem Ruler and Contractual Obligations." *New York University Law Review,* XXXIII, 7, 1958.

Baillie, N. B. E. *Digest of Moohummudan Law,* Parts I and II. London, 1869–75.

Bercher, L. *La Risala par Ibn Abi Zayd al-Qayrawani: Texte et traduction, etc.* Algiers, 1945.

Bercher, L., and Bousquet, G. H. *Le statut personnel en droit musulman hanefite: Texte et traduction annotée du Mukhtasar d'al-Quduri.* Tunis, 1952.

Bousquet, G. H. *Le droit musulman par les textes.* Algiers, 1947.

——. *Du droit musulman et de son application dans le monde.* Algiers, 1949.

——. *Précis de droit musulman, principalement malekite et algérien* (3rd edition). Algiers, 1950.

——. "Abrégé de la loi musulmane selon le rite de l'imam al-Chafi'i par Abou Chodja." *Revue Algérienne, Tunisienne et Marocaine de Législation et de Jurisprudence,* 1935.

Bousquet, G. H., and Berque, J. *Recueil de la loi Musulmane de Zaid ben Ali.* Algiers, 1941.

Brunschvig, R. "De la filiation maternelle en droit Musulman." *Studia Islamica,* 9, 1958.

Colomer, A. *Le code du statut personnel tunisien.* Algiers, 1957.

Coulson, N. J. "Doctrine and Practice in Islamic Law." *Bulletin of the School of Oriental and African Studies,* XVIII, 2, 1956.

——. "The Reform of Family Law in Pakistan." *Studia Islamica,* VII, 1957.

——. "The State and the Individual in Islamic Law." *The International and Comparative Law Quarterly,* 1957.

Fagnan, E. *Risala, ou traité abrégé de droit Malekite et morale Musulmane: Traduction avec commentaire et index analytique.* Paris, 1914.

——. *Les statuts gouvernementaux ou règles de droit public et administratif.* The Ahkam Sultaniya of Mawardi, translated and annotated. Algiers, 1915.

Fyzee, A. A. A. *Outlines of Muhammadan Law* (2nd edition). London, 1955.

———. "Law and Religion in Islam." *Journal of the Bombay Branch of the Royal Asiatic Society*, N.S., 28, 1953.

Gaudefroy-Demombynes, M. *Muslim Institutions*. Translated into English by J. P. Macgregor. London, 1950.

———. "Notes sur l'histoire de l'organisation judiciaire en pays d'Islam." *Revue des études islamiques*, 13, 2, 1939.

Gawad, M. A. *L'exécution testamentaire en droit Musulman*. Paris, 1926.

Gibb, H. A. R. *Mohammedanism* (2nd edition). London, 1953.

———. *Modern Trends in Islam*. Chicago, 1954.

Goldziher, I. *Le dogme et les lois de l'Islam*. Translated into French by F. Arin. Paris, 1920.

Haar, B. ter. *Adat Law in Indonesia*. Translated from the Dutch by E. A. Hoebel and A. A. Schiller. New York, 1948.

Hamilton, C. *The Hedaya* (2nd edition, ed. by S. C. Grady). Translation into English of al-Marghinani's *Hidaya*. London, 1870.

Howard, E. C. *Minhaj et talibin*. Translation into English of L. W. C. Van den Berg's translation into Dutch of al-Nawawi's *Minhaj*. London, 1914.

Juynboll, T. W. "Law (Muhammadan)." *Hastings' Encyclopaedia of Religion and Ethics*, VII.

Khadduri, M. *War and Peace in the Law of Islam*. Baltimore, 1955.

Khadduri, M., and Liebesny, H. (eds.). *Law in the Middle East*. Washington, 1955.

Klein, F. A. *The Religion of Islam*. Madras, 1906.

Knox-Mawer, R. "Islamic Domestic Law in the Colony of Aden." *The International and Comparative Law Quarterly*, October, 1956.

Lammens, H. *L'Islam: croyances et institutions*. Beirut, 1926. Translated into English (*Islam: Beliefs and Institutions*) by E. Denison Ross. London, 1929.

Levy, R. *The Social Structure of Islam.* Cambridge, 1957.

Liebesny, H. J. "Religious Law and Westernization in the Moslem Near East." *American Journal of Comparative Law,* II, 1953.

Linant de Bellefonds, Y. "La suppression des juridictions de statut personnel en Egypte." *Revue internationale de droit comparé,* 1956, No. 3.

———. "Le droit Musulman et le nouveau code civil Egyptien." *Annales juridiques, politiques, économiques et sociales,* 1956, No. 4.

Macdonald, D. B. *Muslim Theology, Jurisprudence and Constitutional Theory.* New York, 1903.

Mahmassani, S. "Muslims: Decadence and Renaissance. Adaptation of Islamic Jurisprudence to Modern Social Needs." *The Muslim World,* XLIV, 1954.

Milliot, Louis. *Travaux de la semaine internationale de droit Musulman.* Paris, 1951.

———. *Introduction à l'étude du droit Musulman.* Paris, 1953.

Mossadegh, M. *Le testament en droit Musulman.* Paris, 1914.

Querry, A. *Droit musulman. Recueil de lois concernant les Musulmans Schyites.* Paris, 1871.

Roussier, J. *Le code tunisien du statut personnel.* Paris, 1957.

———. *L'Annulation du mariage vicié en droit musulman malekite et le sort de la dot.* Algiers, 1956.

Rumsey, A. (ed.). *Al-Sirajiyyah or the Mahommedan Law of Inheritance* (2nd edition). Edition with notes and appendix of Sir William Jones's translation into English. London, 1890.

Ruxton, F. H. *Maliki law.* A summary from French translations of *Mukhtasar Sidi Khalil.* London, 1916.

Santillana, David. "Law and Society." *The Legacy of Islam* (ed. Sir Thomas Arnold and A. Guillaume). London, 1931.

Schacht, J. *The Origins of Muhammadan Jurisprudence.* Oxford, 1950.

———. "Esquisse d'une histoire du droit musulman. Traduit de l'anglais par Jeanne et Félix Arin." Institut des Hautes-Etudes Marocaines: Notes et Documents, XI. Paris, 1952.

Schacht, J. "Islamic Law." *Encyclopaedia of the Social Sciences,* VIII. New York, 1932–7.

——. "Foreign Elements in Ancient Islamic Law." *Journal of Comparative Legislation and International Law,* 32, 1950.

——. "The Law." *Unity and Variety in Muslim Civilization* (ed. G. E. von Grunebaum). Chicago, 1955.

——. "Droit Byzantine et droit Musulman." *Accademia Nazionale dei Lincei.* Rome, 1957.

Seignette, N. *Code musulman.* Translation of Khalil. Paris-Algiers, 1878.

Snouck Hurgronje, C. *Selected Works.* Edited in English and French by G. H. Bousquet and J. Schacht. Leiden, 1957.

——. "Le droit Musulman." *Revue de l'Histoire des Religions,* XXXVII, 1898.

Snoussi, M. T. Es-. *Code du statut personnel (annoté)* (2nd edition). Tunis, 1958.

Symposium on Muslim law, A. Reprinted from *The George Washington Law Review.* Washington, 1953.

Tritton, A. S. "Non-Muslim Subjects of the Muslim State." *Journal of the Royal Asiatic Society,* 1942.

Tyan, Emile. *Histoire de l'organisation judiciaire en pays d'Islam.* Two volumes. Paris, 1938–43.

——. *Le notariat et le regime de la preuve par écrit dans le pratique du droit musulman.* Beirut, 1945 (Annales de l'ecole Française de Droit de Beyrouth, No. 2, 1954).

——. *Institutions du droit public Musulman.* Paris, 1954–6.

Van den Berg, L. W. C. *Minhaj at talibin: texte arabe avec traduction et annotations.* Three volumes. Batavia, 1882–4.

Vesey-FitzGerald, S. *Muhammadan Law.* London, 1931.

Wilson, R. K. *Anglo-Muhammadan Law* (6th edition). Calcutta, 1930.